# Sheep

John Mark Gray

ISBN-13: 979-8-6909-1612-1

# DEDICATION

I would like to dedicate this book to all the corrupt and incompetent politicians, the material practically wrote itself!

# CONTENTS


1   Introduction                              1

2   CNN & Fox News                           13

3   Divisive Country                         29

4   Race & Politics                          45

5   Politics Makes Everything Worse          59

6   The Business of Politics                 71

7   Lobbying & Corruption                    83

8   Voting Doesn't Matter                   105

9   The Same Old Thing                      123

10  Conclusion – Freedom & Democracy        151

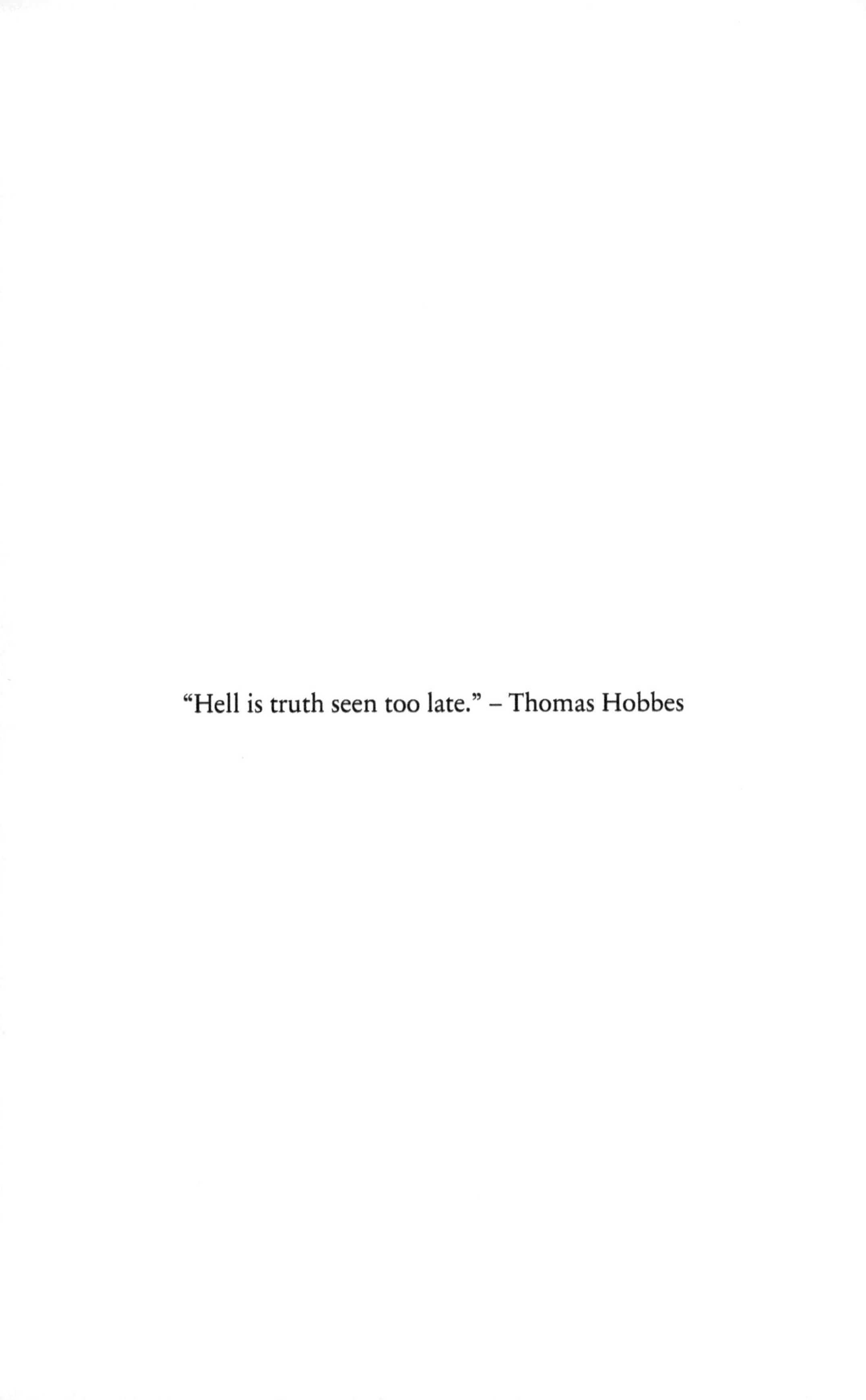

"Hell is truth seen too late." – Thomas Hobbes

# 1 INTRODUCTION

I will start this book with a brief introduction into my political affiliations, beliefs and mindset going into this work. I am apolitical which means that I am rather more objective regarding political matters than most people in this country and perhaps the rest of the world for that matter.

I am not a Republican, Democrat or an Independent. In fact, I have never identified with any particular political party in my lifetime. I am interested in issues that impact this country and naturally me personally as a rational human being and citizen of the United States of America.

It is apparent that many of these issues are highly politicized in nature. However, I stick to examining the actual issues themselves and not the politics behind these often-heated matters. Just like I would examine any problem and proposed solution that I encounter in trying to live my best possible and most successful life as a human being on this planet.

I have never voted in a political election at any level. Unlike most people in America, I realized rather quickly that voting makes no meaningful difference in this country. This is despite the vast voting rhetoric and propaganda spewed out in my lifetime from politicians, online message boards, community leaders, fellow citizens, athletic superstars and the likes of MTV and Hollywood celebrities.

I am rather skeptical regarding the American political system ever changing enough to have legitimate elections where my voting would make any tangible and meaningful difference in this country. So I doubt that I will ever vote during my lifetime, and I will never be voting just for the sake of appearances.

This all makes me rather objective as a person to analyze the American political system, evaluate the current state of the institution as a whole, determine what ails it, and make unbiased and nonpartisan recommendations for improving upon this governing system. I realize there may be some readers who believe the American political system works just fine and doesn't need to be changed at all, and hopefully I can make some inroads into this flawed way of thinking on the matter.

We just finished another political election cycle in this country with Joe Biden winning the national election over Donald Trump by an extremely narrow margin.[1] The election was so close that there are recounts occurring as I write this portion of the book, and in practice, the election results were still being contested in the courts. The basic breakdown of the election results is that the Republicans carried the majority of the states in the center of the country, and the Democrats secured the states along the two coasts of the nation.

This is hardly a surprise as the election winner is basically determined by a handful of swing states in today's highly

---

[1] https://www.nytimes.com/interactive/2020/11/03/us/elections/results-president.html

partisan and overly divisive political environment. In many of these swing states the election results ended up being very close, and it wouldn't take much to swing these election results in either direction. In short, America is a highly divided country politically speaking, and political views seem to fall along the party lines of the Two-Party System in the United States.

This basic political split in the country along party lines has been a noticeable trend, with landslide election results being few and far between, and slim mandates are often reversed by the subsequent mid-term elections, as it takes less than two years for the American people to have voter's remorse.

To say that the American political system is highly dysfunctional is an understatement in my mind. Not only does the country seem to be trapped in a never-ending political morass tantamount to being stuck in quicksand. The political system fundamentally just doesn't serve the needs of Americans these days. The American political system is as broken as a political system can be while still having most Americans actively participating and believing in the legitimacy of the overall political system itself.

I will offer some suggestions for improving upon the system in what could be called some minor changes to the political process, to some medium level changes which will make a profound difference in the effectiveness and performance of the political system as a whole, all the way to the more extreme changes that I suggest for completely reforming and revolutionizing the entire American political system.

In some sense I am being pragmatic and a realist regarding change, as it takes a lot to get countries, governments, and people to change their way of thinking, behaving, and acting. Let alone asking them to make major changes in the way their government works, the political process itself, and completely overhauling the American political system.

But even if most of my suggestions are rejected as too extreme in favor of a desperate clinging to the broken status quo, maybe enough small improvements can be made to upgrade some aspects of the American political system so that it performs better and leads to slightly more competent outcomes for citizens of the country.

Now let me make some stronger points here. The American people are going to have to start learning from their previous mistakes and stop acting like a bunch of mindless sheep that are absolutely being taken advantage of by the Two-Party System. The American voters are being tricked by the political drama and theatre, as both political parties are doing them no good in Washington.

Moreover, it is my stronger assertion that the American voters are just not capable of making wise political choices. So the political process itself needs to be changed, as the results speak for themselves over the last 70 years.

I will say that this is a political ideas book, and there should be a little bit of something for everyone who reads *Sheep*. This is regardless of political affiliation, as the book has no underlying hidden agenda in that respect.

The main purpose of the book is to get people to start thinking about ways to improve the American political system, as it is definitely in need of some major changes right now. However, it might be helpful to leave some of your ideological and political baggage behind as you read *Sheep*, with the intention of having a more open-minded approach to change itself.

As I mentioned earlier, we have been steadily trending

towards more and more political divisiveness as a country, and a lot of this political divide stems from the invasiveness and outright propaganda incessantly churned out by the brainwashing machines of the two-party political system.

As a result, everyone in America thinks they know what is right politically speaking. This is regardless of educational levels, overall intelligence, practical common sense, logical reasoning abilities and worldly sophistication. In a nutshell, American politics is a hobby and sport for all, anybody can play this game.

The problem is Americans are just not that knowledgeable about the inner workings of politics in general, and specifically the American political system. In all honesty, most Americans are very poor at playing this game of politics, and they just make absolutely terrible voters. This is pretty much across the board, regardless of age group, educational background, political affiliation, professional status, and social class as American citizens.

This is important because there are a lot of problems right now in America, and what we have been doing for the last 70 years isn't working. The country is definitely on a downward trajectory from an overall quality of life standpoint, and this decline started as early as the 1960s epoch.

The United States has dropped the ball in so many areas from education, healthcare, mental health, business development, infrastructure investment, military management, government regulation, and fiscal policymaking to list just some of the patently obvious systemic failures and problems facing the nation.

The general quality of life and mental well-being of the American citizen has been on a steady decline as witnessed by and embodied in the lower purchasing power and overall decrease in the standard of living produced through employment and wages for the average middle-class citizen in this country. We hit the peak for this metric in the 1950s and have been on a steady and unending decline ever since as a nation.

But probably even more worrisome is the fact that America really seems to be getting dumber as a country, as there is a whole lot of "stupid" right now in this nation. For instance, if leaders that the country holds up as important people to listen to in the fields of business, entertainment, music, and politics are in any way a reflection of our society, then this says a lot about the overall competence and intelligence of America as a whole. The United States of America really is a vacuously broken culture which lacks any notion of common sense and is absolutely being left behind on the global stage.

We are going to have to change the way we do things as a society, change the way we think as a community, and start working together to solve problems instead of the current status quo where half the country is constantly battling with the other half over some rather unimportant differences when taken into the broader context of having and maintaining a healthy functioning and competitive democracy on the world stage.

For example, the American people have been brainwashed and manipulated to take sides on issues where there should be no real disagreements if it wasn't in the best interests of the Two-Party System. The Two-Party System is used to promote divisiveness and market distinct differences to create artificial debates and hostilities amongst the people.

This divisive state of affairs is good for business and the going concern of the two-party political system in America. All of which preserves and perpetuates the incompetent status quo and the never-ending morass of the next election cycle where future money and power is accrued for both political parties.

In case you haven't figured it out by now, politics is a business first and foremost in this country. It is my contention that for the good of the nation, politics should not be a thriving business and lucrative industry in its own right. But make no mistake about it, our current Two-Party System of Republicans and Democrats is a booming business enterprise.

These two political parties represent giant corporations similar to that of Apple and Microsoft. In fact, American politics is really all about money and power when you delve into the underlying business model of this political paradigm, and certainly not what is in the best interests and common good of Americans and the country as a whole.

The American people need to wake up out of their 70 years long slumber because not only has the American government gotten far too big and intrusive, but the political system itself has become the ultimate corporate monopoly. Every year the government and the Two-Party System gains more control over the lives of ordinary Americans, and this is not in a good and healthy way.

These giant business entities are so intertwined with the overall national government, that they hold each other upright like two drunks after the bars have long since closed in the city. These two political behemoths effectively rely on each other to continue the entire charade that we call a functioning political democracy.

Both the Two-Party System and the Federal Government continue to gain more power, take in more money, and are growing like giant Blobs in old horror movies.[2] These dual American institutions have become lazy, obese, massively incompetent, and morally bankrupt giant bureaucracies representing hopelessly inefficient and thoroughly corrupt Blobs of fiction.

The prime culprit responsible for this grim state of affairs is the American citizen and voter who has become intellectually lazy, fat and happy with incompetence and mediocrity, and remarkably ignorant regarding both historical political truths and the failed government policies of their representatives in Washington over the last 70 years.

These voters have embraced the dysfunctional Two-Party System like sports teams that they need to support and cheer for in a patriotic and emotional manner, all this at the expense of intellectual integrity. In short, the American voters have embraced stupidity in all its unremarkable splendor, and you can see this in the way they idolize the dumbest people who get the most attention in our society through a multitude of antisocial, uncivilized, and culturally impoverished behaviors.

It is quite evident that social media and the overall media industry as a whole helped perpetuate this downward spiral of choosing emotional "feel-goodism" over intellectual rigor and integrity as human beings. However, make no mistake, the country as a whole has made this same apathetic and lazy choice to reject knowledge, critical reasoning, intelligence, and rationality as a means towards sound political thought, discussion, and ideals.

As a result of this conscious choice by the American people,

---

[2] https://en.wikipedia.org/wiki/The_Blob;
https://www.criterion.com/films/630-the-blob;
https://www.rottentomatoes.com/m/the_blob_1988

this has definitely set the stage for being taken advantage of and ripped off by the political class in this country. It is obvious at this point that the American voters are helpless to defend themselves against these career politicians who have essentially raped and pillaged their emotionally based minds to the point of being brainless, unthinking subservient participants in the political process.

Consequently, this country would benefit from term limits to help restrain these exploitative career politicians who are working the broken political system like the professional grifters that they have dedicated their lives to becoming as despicable human beings. Additionally, the educational system needs to do a better job of helping and laying the groundwork for improved decision-making and critical reasoning skillsets by the American voters.

For instance, even at the best colleges and universities in America, most students have no idea who is head of the Federal Reserve, and what role they play in their current government. The Federal Reserve is probably the single most powerful functioning entity right now in this country. The Federal Reserve is an unelected body of economic policymakers which is largely unchecked and has more influence on Americans' wellbeing than any politician in Washington, including the President of the United States.

It is quite apparent that Americans in general need to be better educated about the inner workings of government, because right now most American voters get their political views from the propaganda channels of the Two-Party System, the political entertainment shows masquerading as journalism, and social media. It is no wonder they make terrible political decisions with these obviously flawed informational inputs.

In truth, Americans need to learn how to think for themselves instead of acting like a bunch of mindless sheep who fanatically idolize athletes, celebrities, and entertainers in society who tell them what to believe about political issues. There is no positive correlation between any of these professional careers and making intelligent, highly reflective, critically thinking, and well-informed political decisions.

Given our current unsustainable state of affairs, Americans should not be looking for and taking political advice from unintelligent people in society, and unfortunately there are a lot of unintelligent people that are held up as bastions of knowledge and authorities on political issues here in America these days.

This untenable set of circumstances has all contributed to the American public in general, and specifically the American voters being politically illiterate as a body. Basically a flock of stupid unthinking sheep that the Two-Party System and career politicians have avariciously and ruthlessly exploited to no end.

These political opportunists have enriched themselves with enormous wealth and power along the way, and undoubtedly have little remorse for the American voters who are absolutely being taking advantage of by this thoroughly unfortunate state of affairs in our broken political system.

This is why I picked this particular title for the book. I was trying to decide between *No Hope for Humanity* and *Sheep* as the two prospective titles. In the end, I chose the title based upon the factor most responsible for America's broken political system.

The American people and the voting public really are best characterized as Sheep. This flock of intellectually myopic and unthinking *Sheep* are definitely being exploited and manipulated by the dysfunctional and severely flawed political system that we refer to as a Democracy.

# 2 CNN & FOX NEWS

The News Business has quite a storied history in the United States, as many famous and wealthy people have built their personal legacies through this medium of packaging, selling, and spreading information.

I will pick up the story with what I refer to as the end of the true journalism era with the retiring of Walter Cronkite, who effectively retired from full-time journalism in March of 1981.[3] This journalistic icon retiring occurred around the same time that cable television in this country was really picking up steam with the Cable News Network (CNN) coming on air in June 1980.[4]

This point in time marks a sort of methodological and philosophical shift in the way people received, viewed, and thought about the news. This created a power shift from the basic monopolies of the three major networks broadcasting the news with their giant and highly profitable news organizations

---

[3] https://en.wikipedia.org/wiki/Walter_Cronkite
[4] https://www.history.com/this-day-in-history/cnn-launches; https://en.wikipedia.org/wiki/CNN

to a dynamic where consumers could literally get their news on demand from CNN twenty-four hours a day.

As advertising dollars moved to cable television and there were more outlets available for consumers to receive the news, the overall quality and standards of the news business were compromised in the end. This is because when there are essentially news monopolies at the major networks, there is more of a focus on journalistic standards along with overall integrity and less a concern about the business aspects of the news product.

When cable news came to the forefront, everyone in the news business started getting squeezed as the news ecosystem and supply chains were markedly disrupted, opening up more competition for the same pie of advertising dollars.

This increased competition puts pressure on news ratings, as journalistic standards and integrity become a luxury in the modern era of cable television where the chase and fight for ratings brings business drivers to the forefront of both journalism and the news industry.

This transformation from news being journalism based to that of "Infotainment" in the increasingly hypercompetitive world of the modern news business happens slow at first, but as more competitors basically sell out their news credentials in favor of increased ratings, the transformational changes in the industry pick up speed, to the point where we are today, with the news business being almost unrecognizable from the good old days of Walter Cronkite and the CBS Evening News.

This news ecosystem transformation went hyperbolic once the internet and the digital age evolved, and all bets for actual journalistic integrity and legitimate news journalism standards went out the window and have been forever lost in America.

This is part of the story of how we got here today in the news business, but there is definitely some more background information and political angles that need to be fleshed out in the analysis.

So naturally with more competition, and everyone fighting for ratings, viewers and relevancy in the news business, there started to be a liberal bias which reflected the views and values of the big media markets on the two coasts of the country. Again, when in doubt, always follow the money. This is where the money resides for television networks and the big advertising revenues. Thus, messages are tailored to the markets, they become universalized, and this liberal bias in the news media steadily creeps into the overall end product.

The American people recognized this liberal bias in the news, but it wasn't at the extreme levels like it is today. Where the liberal bias is essentially so skewed and extreme that the news industry has no credibility whatsoever now, as they simply are no longer objective journalists, period.

In this environment, along comes Rush Limbaugh in 1988 with a nationally syndicated radio show which ended up being a reactionary foil to the previously mentioned liberal biases in the national media and news business.[5]

This show was very successful, centered around conservative ideas and values, and created quite a following for Rush Limbaugh. He rose to fame, authored several books, and became a force in the way that politics was covered and followed in the local and national media.

In a sense, Rush Limbaugh was a political trailblazer, as he effectively created and monetized this burgeoning field of

---

[5] https://en.wikipedia.org/wiki/Rush_Limbaugh

Political Entertainment.[6]

Well, remember to always follow the money thread in all of this societal evolution of the American culture, because at the root of all this is money. If somebody can make a buck, you can bet things are about to change in this world.

In point of fact, Rush Limbaugh was so successful at filling this conservative political entertainment niche, i.e., he was making a lot of money for everybody involved in his radio show. It was an enormous success, and everyone in the political news industry took notice of his conservative approach to covering political events in society.

This all led to Rupert Murdoch creating the Fox News Channel in 1996 which also appealed to a conservative audience like Rush Limbaugh.[7] Well, this business venture was like the Rush Limbaugh Show on steroids because cable television has so much more potential for building and scaling an audience of viewers.

And needless to say this business venture was a homerun for Rupert Murdoch as the Fox News Channel attracted a large audience, garnered consistently high ratings, and could charge good advertising rates. In short, the Fox News Channel was great for making money.

Consequently, instead of the news media having an implicit liberal bias, Rush Limbaugh and subsequently Rupert Murdoch and Fox News with the help of Roger Ailes went the next step further and just explicitly made known their conservative and Republican leaning news bias.[8]

---

[6] https://www.rushlimbaugh.com/
[7] https://en.wikipedia.org/wiki/Fox_News; https://www.foxnews.com/
[8] https://en.wikipedia.org/wiki/Roger_Ailes;
https://www.britannica.com/biography/Roger-Ailes

This out in the open approach to obvious news bias not only infuriated the left in this country, but the other political based television shows, news media and journalists in America decided that what was good for *Team Conservative Republican* is good for *Team Liberal Democrat*, so to speak. Concisely, they wanted in on this Explicit Political Bias Money Train.

This looking around the media landscape and seeing what is being rewarded in the marketplace sowed the seeds for where we are today. This inward analysis and reflection by the industry ultimately led to the evolution of the unabashed, unrepentant, and unfettered model of Explicit News Bias and Political Infotainment with the goal of chasing higher ratings regardless of journalistic integrity costs.

This played out in CNN, MSNBC, and many other liberal news media outlets going full throttle with explicit news bias and political infotainment that is meant to promote liberal political ideas and appease a Democratic and left leaning audience of viewers.[9]

In summary, these news organizations would be the anti-Fox News Channel, all with the goal of cashing in on the same level of ratings, viewership numbers, and overall revenues as a basic methodology for how they covered and presented the news.

This is where we are today with Fox News, Rush Limbaugh, and some conservative minded online websites such as Breitbart News, The Federalist and so forth on one side of the political infotainment universe, and CNN, MSNBC, The Huffington Post, Politico, and many others on the liberal side of the political news spectrum.[10]

---

[9] https://en.wikipedia.org/wiki/MSNBC; https://www.msnbc.com/
[10] https://en.wikipedia.org/wiki/Breitbart_News;
https://en.wikipedia.org/wiki/The_Federalist_(website);

But you notice how I used the term political news, as all news today is political, and theatrically produced and packaged with a definite audience in mind.[11]

The end result is that there is no more objective and principled news in America which is free from political bias and informational spin. All the major news organizations have morphed or devolved into partisan propaganda machines for the Two-Party System of Liberal Democrats and Conservative Republicans.

The money part of the equation is rather predictable and even cynically expected in this day and age. However, the journalism schools at major universities should be ashamed of themselves for their role in churning out an entire generation of non-journalists and partisan propaganda artists whose only real motivation is chasing the almighty dollar.

Just look at the journalism courses offered in academia, and you will find this underlying theme of chasing ratings at all costs running through these degree programs. The ultimate goal is to push and strive for high ratings in this wonderful world of shaping political narratives, creating artificial controversies, fueling overall divisiveness, pushing political agendas, and projecting sensationalized conflict into every news story.

The days of just giving the objective and unbiased facts in reporting the news is simply too boring and unprofitable. The old school journalism model just doesn't bring in the necessary advertising revenue according to modern journalistic standards and profitability theory taught in journalism programs. The

---

https://en.wikipedia.org/wiki/HuffPost;
https://en.wikipedia.org/wiki/Politico
[11] https://www.pewresearch.org/topics/political-polarization/;
https://www.journalism.org/2014/10/21/political-polarization-media-habits/

main job of journalism today is to create the news, and it sure isn't simply to report the actual facts of the matter, that isn't news according to their religion.

It really is appalling that the entire academic and professional industry of journalism has sold out their integrity and journalistic standards to the gods of big business, corporate interests, and political parties. Hence, legitimate journalistic principles regarding objective facts and unbiased news which isn't shaped for economic and political gain, no longer exists anywhere in the United States of America.

This chain of events in the news industry has some negative consequences for our society as a whole. First of all, CNN and Fox News are brainwashing viewers and conditioning them to believe in patently false, utterly stupid, and demonstrably illogical thoughts and ideas on a regular basis.

And most Americans are just not well equipped to offset the negative and corrosive effects of this pernicious political propaganda promulgated by an unprincipled and ethically challenged news media with its highly destructive disinformation machinery and unscrupulously manipulative marketing practices.

In real terms, the news media have completely corrupted the minds of most Americans.

Another problem for the news industry is that news anchors themselves need to be actual journalists instead of entertainment hosts. It would be better for the industry as a whole if they got rid of the stereotypical bubble headed bleached blondes who would be better served as entertainment reporters or selling cosmetics on home shopping channels as opposed to covering and providing news along with inane, simpleminded political commentary. We definitely need more plainer looking, intelligent people who are legitimate journalists in the news industry.

However, the Two-Party System is loving this wretched state of affairs in the news business, as they have giant propaganda machines pushing out their political agendas and recruiting new cult members for their parties. Yes, the political parties have taken on many characteristics similar to highly destructive cults where participants have literally lost all ability to think for themselves anymore.

The main takeaway from this sad situation stands that there is no credibility in the News Industry and the field of Journalism whatsoever these days. In fact, the misinformation and blatant partisan propaganda is so bad right now that there needs to be a tobacco like warning label or banner that runs across all these news outlets and their respective platforms. This news disclaimer should read something like the following: "This is not objective, fact-based news; this is Political Info-Entertainment and may be harmful for your understanding of political events!"

But it is obvious that many people in our society buy into this political propaganda churned out by the news industry, and it definitely affects the manner in which they view events, think about political issues, and interact with each other in society.

There are without doubt some serious and dangerous ramifications for our country being an effectively functioning Democracy, all because a bunch of unscrupulous people in the News Industry wanted to make more money and sold out their journalistic principles along the way.

The symbiotic relationship that has evolved between the Two-Party System and the News Business all in the pursuit of financial gain, has meant that most Americans walk around thinking like conditioned cult members as opposed to informed citizens about the important political issues facing this nation right now.

Ironically, in this age of information most people are purposely fed false and misleading information on such a regular basis that America is actually resembling unmistakable similarities to the Russian and Chinese propaganda machines of Joseph Stalin and Mao Zedong.[12]

It is ironic because when I was growing up in this country, we routinely criticized China and Russia for this type of deplorable propaganda, and that America was built upon cherished democratic ideals such as having freedom of speech, a fair and objective press, and discovery and promotion of fact-based journalistic principles. If you cannot trust the news in a country, then you effectively have no country. In essence, you are no longer a free and democratic nation.

It is obvious that the only real winners with this current untrustworthy news paradigm are the political parties of the Two-Party System, as this political propaganda serves as recruitment tools for their politics and general business development needs. It should be self-evident that this problematic state of affairs in the News Industry is remarkably destructive for objective and rational thinking on behalf of the voting public in America.

The News and Journalism Industry needs to be politically independent, and not politically biased and motivated, just like a good brain surgeon or heart doctor, they don't bring politics into the operating room, as it is highly unethical and

---

[12] https://en.wikipedia.org/wiki/Joseph_Stalin;
https://en.wikipedia.org/wiki/Mao_Zedong

antithetical to the basic principles of their craft. These doctors have a moral obligation to take care of patients in an unbiased and objective manner, well the same goes for the news business, just present the news in an unbiased and objective manner.

You should have an unwavering ethical code, which was instilled in you from journalism school to live by this basic journalistic principle of being objective and unbiased. But unfortunately the Education Industry itself has now become a business, as colleges and universities have long since lost any notion of objective integrity, ethical values, and professional standards. These institutions sold their academic souls to the political devil a long time ago.

Therefore, if the News and Journalism Industry cannot find their moral compass, and just report the basic facts in delivering and presenting the news of the day, basically letting the readers and viewers decide what these facts mean for themselves, then these news organizations need to have their broadcasting licenses revoked and their journalistic privileges taken away by the courts and the regulatory bodies in this country.[13]

Moreover, if the existing overwatch function doesn't fit the current state of the News Industry because these are antiquated checks and balances today, then we need to create an independent, objective News and Journalism overwatch function in society. This overwatch function would have the authority to impose standards on the industry, and failure to act as a responsible news organization would mean that your journalistic license is subject to forfeiture.

Why should the News Industry be outside of government

---

[13] https://www.fcc.gov/media/radio/public-and-broadcasting; https://www.supremecourt.gov/; https://en.wikipedia.org/wiki/Media_regulation

regulation just like any other industry in America? The News and Journalism Industry had the opportunity to self-regulate their behaviors and actions and failed miserably in this regard. These kinds of results are similar to most organizations and industries who are not held accountable to any regulatory body or oversight committee, as in the end, the honor system always fails in the world of big business.

Do we expect investment banks to act appropriately and self-regulate their own behaviors and practices? Of course we don't, then why should the News Business be any different. In reality, human beings and industries on the whole have demonstrated that eventually they will cross ethical boundaries when it comes to making money, as they just cannot be trusted to act in the best interests of society on principle alone.

Unfortunately, the News and Journalism Industry has reached this point where they can no longer be trusted to monitor themselves and self-regulate their activities and behaviors. It has become abundantly clear that an independent third party in the federal government needs to get involved in monitoring and regulating their unscrupulous business practices.

This is truly a sad day in America, but this is what the news and journalism profession has become today by being left to their own devices, as the industry as a whole plainly sold out their journalistic souls to chase the money.

It is time for the News and Journalism Industry to reassert objective, fact-based journalistic principles into the News which are free of political biases, party affiliations, and ratings motivated agendas. This should be a public service mandate on behalf of the entire News and Journalism Industry in this country, as trustworthy news is essential for having and maintaining a healthy democracy.

In general terms, I am the last person who wants more government influence, intervention, and regulation, as government already has an enormously big impact on many areas of Americans' lives. So hopefully the pendulum will swing back the other way, and the free market guided by the American people will start rewarding objective, fact-based news and journalism in the marketplace.

Then this will incentivize the big money and advertising dollars to follow suit, thereby punishing the purveyors of Political News Infotainment currently masquerading as journalism which blatantly promotes and propagandizes the agendas of the Two-Party System with cult like devotion.

I realize that a lot of journalists and people in the news media believe that the ends of their sacred political parties justify a lot of the unprincipled means they utilize to propagandize the news. However, not only are these people just talking their respective political books, but have so completely lost their way, that they fail to realize the sacrificing of much larger principles in the process.

And I repeat, a country that cannot rely on independent, fact-based news, which is free from political influence, is a second-rate country on the cultural, moral, and social decline. Furthermore, the converse of this statement applies as well regarding societies trying to evolve into better, first-rate countries which have objective and trustworthy news organizations.

A couple other notes on this subject, it is evident and one of the recurring themes of this book, that the failure of the American education system is making citizens very vulnerable to propaganda in general.

The American citizenry seems to have lost their ability to think critically about most issues from more than one perspective, and this makes them perfect targets for the propaganda machines of the News and Journalism Industry which ultimately just reinforces the power and influence of the Two-Party System in this country.

The platforms of social media similarly need to be classified much better along this news versus political entertainment continuum. It is also noteworthy that these social media companies have been actively engaged in censorship practices which are politically motivated over the last couple of election cycles.

This is an important issue right now considering the fact that these social media platforms with their monopolistic standing which provides them enormous reach and power have become significant political influencers in elections these days.

These social media platforms have become the de facto arbiters of political truth in America, and much of this is highly arbitrary and thoroughly subjective on their behalf, and certainly reeks of political favoritism.

If you are going to be a conservative or liberal shill for the political parties, then you need to be labeled as such because the American citizenry just doesn't have the requisite critical thinking and analytical evaluation skills to ascertain that they are being manipulated like a flock of naïve little sheep by these social media platforms.

I don't believe that religious organizations should be involved in politics, as I think the separation between church and state is a good principle to uphold. In fact, all businesses should employ this strategy as well because most things are made worse by politics.

Furthermore, I think that many of these businesses and public figures in the worlds of entertainment, social media, and sports will learn the hard way that being partisan propaganda puppets for the Two-Party System is just not a good business model to follow over the long run.

Simply put, this politically motivated partisan approach is downright bad for business, especially when you consider that the country is split right down the middle along the party lines of the two-party political system.

Consequently, you are alienating and turning off half of your potential customer base, and both political parties represent rather large customer bases to offend. Unfortunately, many businesses will learn this fundamental truism far too late to do anything about it.

This all goes hand in hand to negatively impact the world that we live in today. We have CNN and Fox News serving out political propaganda by the boatloads, as the gullible American citizenry which are best characterized as a bunch of unthinking Sheep are being politically brainwashed at an alarming and unprecedented rate in our society.

All the while these mindless Sheep become fired up with immense fervor and passion to join up and connect with their fellow cult members in the Two-Party System to fight against their mortal political enemies by searching for and validating any slight differences to justify their whole existence as members of the two political teams.

This self-fulfilling, highly destructive, and counterproductive feedback loop just further spreads divisiveness in America, and strictly reinforces the cultish dominance and power of the two political parties in this country.

It is little wonder this country is so screwed up right now, with half the citizens thinking the other half are complete idiots for their political beliefs. Frankly, I am on the outside looking in at this whole political paradigm, and I am telling the American people that you are all a bunch of foolish, unwise Sheep.

It is obvious that the American political system is broken and needs to be changed significantly in order to produce better outcomes for its citizens in the future. And fundamentally, this means getting the News and Journalism Industry out of the business of partisan politics.

The News and Journalism Industry needs a reawakening of purpose, as they need to get back to providing unbiased, objective fact-based news which is trustworthy. This will be necessary if America is ever going to right its sinking ship and start working towards being a first-rate country on the world stage once again.

# 3 DIVISIVE COUNTRY

I t is hard to get people to agree on much of anything these days, but when it comes to politics there is actually considerable agreement, it is just split depending upon which team or political party people have adopted as their own. Another more cynical way to describe this social activity is that Americans are effectively recruited through rigorous behavioral conditioning and propaganda campaigns on behalf of the Two-Party System in this country.

This starts at the grass roots level, and the Two-Party System has tentacles that reach far and wide into even the smallest communities within each state. In point of fact, think in terms of the Catholic Church in Rome here as a historical model for this type of influence with the goal of broadening the political power base through growing foundational roots into these small communities like a giant partisan tree spanning the nation.

As a result of this highly partisan state of affairs in America, unsurprisingly, even the local city council members are all party affiliated and pushing the largely propagandist messages of the

Republican and Democratic parties.[14] Additionally, the campaign fundraising money in these local municipalities as it happens often comes from powerful and wealthy political donors at the elite levels of American society.[15]

The mayors in all of these American cities are likewise participating in the Two-Party System and receive considerable financial and logistical support from the dominant political parties along the way.

This dynamic gains steam as you move to the level of state legislatures, government officials and governors in each state. Moreover, these political races and positions are all heavily influenced by the vast resources, organizational support, political reach, and overall breadth of the Two-Party System in America.

All these different levels flow up like the classic pyramid marketing scheme regarding the general structure of each lower political level tying in nicely and supporting the level above it with increased resources, fundraising possibilities, money, and power.

Hence, all the hard work at the grass roots level in each city, county, regional district, and state for the Republican and Democratic parties rolls up nicely and sets the political table with regard to the national level for these two partisan behemoths.

This is what makes it a political duopoly, because these two parties control every aspect of the American political system. In

---

[14] https://en.wikipedia.org/wiki/Houston_City_Council; https://en.wikipedia.org/wiki/Portland,_Maine_City_Council
[15] https://ballotpedia.org/George_Soros/Political_activity; https://ballotpedia.org/Michael_Bloomberg; https://ballotpedia.org/Charles_Koch

other words, good luck in trying to get a third party off the ground in this country. It just takes considerable developmental and financial resources, and the politically entrenched partisan roots run far too deep to meaningfully upset the ingrained status quo of the Two-Party System in America.

There have been many attempts to get a third party up and running as a viable alternative to this highly polarizing political duopoly, and these have largely failed to make significant inroads that prospered and were sustainable over the long term. In brief, these efforts failed to make any substantive, long-term difference in the structure of the American political system.

In point of fact, the Two-Party System, led busily by both the Republican and Democratic parties practically bands together to sabotage any third party from getting off the ground or gaining a meaningful foothold into the American political system via many exclusionary methods and strategies.

These political behemoths realize that a viable third party takes money and power away from both parties in the end. Therefore, like worker bees protecting the queen bee, both political parties send out the defense forces to eradicate and sabotage any third party from being a major competitor and legitimate threat to their anticompetitive, duopolistic business model.

It is interesting that the two political parties actually like and benefit from having a political foe in the other party that they can demonize in good and evil terms like biblical narratives to contrast themselves from The Dark Side of the opposing political party. Thus, two political parties are good for business, however, having three, four and five legitimate political parties where the American voters have true alternatives is just not a good thing in their minds.

Well here we are stuck with a political duopoly that is so thoroughly entrenched into this country that most Americans fail to realize how their political viewpoints are being conditioned and manipulated by the far-reaching political tentacles of the Two-Party System like giant Democratic and Republican Octopuses.

This vast political infrastructure all rolls up and supports the top of the political ecosystem at the national level with the political campaigns of the House of Representatives, the Senate, and the President of the United States.

Now one gets a sense of just how much money and power is at stake in each election cycle, and why the federal government just continues to get bigger each and every year. This occurs regardless of whether we can actually support this government through conventional tax receipts. In the final analysis, the business of politics itself is what really drives all of this activity and ultimately runs the show in Washington.

This is all one giant bureaucracy supported by the political rivers of money and power that flow from local municipalities all the way up through the state governments, eventually leading to the bigger tributaries that run off into Washington, D.C. It is effectively a veritable cesspool, an incestuous bureaucratic swamp, a criminal organization, political duopoly, and pyramid marketing scheme which ultimately represents the big business nature of government politics.

However you want to label it makes little difference, as the lesson to be gleaned here is that Americans essentially have no chance of making a difference by voting and participating in the political process. This business of politics and its corrupt ecosystem is what the American people are up against which ultimately reduces them to being merely spectators in the political parade.

The system itself has taken over, and it really doesn't matter which party you vote for in America, as in, *Meet the new boss, same as the old boss* to quote from The Who's song, "Won't Get Fooled Again."[16]

These political parties may promote themselves according to virtuous ideals, and even market themselves as the "Good" versus the "Evil" in stark contrast with the other party, but this is all an illusory trick presented with artful deception like a great magician fools the uninitiated audience. This magic show mesmerizes the American voters who become distracted and divided into political teams like a bunch of dozy sheep waiting to be slaughtered.

These bedazzled voters receive a healthy dose of false and illusory self-identity in the process which paradoxically gives their bleak and incoherent lives a sense of ephemeral purpose. However, the system itself never changes and continues along the same path of not only preserving, but relentlessly growing the giant bureaucracy of the continually failing status quo in Washington.

This is why the Washington, D.C. metropolitan area which includes the nation's capital and parts of Maryland and Virginia have some of the highest per capita incomes of anywhere in the country.[17] All living off the endless handouts and massive bureaucracy of our federal government with its evergrowing

---

[16] https://en.wikipedia.org/wiki/Won%27t_Get_Fooled_Again; https://www.azlyrics.com/lyrics/who/wontgetfooledagain.html

[17] https://en.wikipedia.org/wiki/Washington_metropolitan_area; https://en.wikipedia.org/wiki/List_of_United_States_metropolitan_areas_by_per_capita_income; https://www.cnbc.com/2019/03/20/the-highest-earning-region-in-the-us-isnt-in-new-york-or-california.html

satellite business ventures *Inside the Beltway.*

So while Americans are being distracted by the partisan divisiveness of the Two-Party Political System, everyone is being taken for a ride in the process, as the country at large is unquestionably burning to the ground through incompetent mismanagement.

These political pirates are looting the once vast resources of this country while its citizens are too busy fighting against each other to notice this American political tragedy happening on their supposed patriotic watch.

This partisan divisiveness is certainly helpful for the underlying plan of the political pirates, serving as an excellent and effective diversionary tactic, while all the precious gold is literally and figuratively being stolen from the coffers of America. These political bureaucrats are all getting rich, while the average Americans are all becoming poorer as a social and economic class.

It is quite apparent that the country on the whole is poorly run, has massive waste and inefficiencies, and is significantly in debt with no end in sight. Notably, America is heavily mortgaged to foreign nations such as China, Japan, and Europe, and is being artificially propped up by the increasingly risky policy measures of the Federal Reserve.[18]

In truth, America is on the brink of a systemic collapse which will destroy the current economic, social, and political

---

[18] https://en.wikipedia.org/wiki/National_debt_of_the_United_States; https://www.investopedia.com/articles/markets-economy/090616/5-countries-own-most-us-debt.asp; https://www.federalreserve.gov/monetarypolicy/2020-06-mpr-part2.htm; https://www.federalreserve.gov/monetarypolicy/2020-06-mpr-summary.htm

paradigm as we know it.

The American people better wake up really quick from this political divisiveness slumber state that they have been hypnotized into because they are all being taken advantage of and being used by the two political parties in this broken American political system that is mistakenly characterized as a legitimate representative democracy.

It is ironic that with such a divisive country and the Two-Party System marketing themselves as such polar opposites of each other, that in the end, things never change regardless of which party is in power. In the final analysis, it doesn't matter who you vote for, which party wins the given election cycle, we still get the exact same political outcomes from our government in Washington.

This is why voting doesn't truly matter despite all the theatrical hype, political propaganda, and hysterical drama of demonizing politics. In reality, the lobbyists, special interest groups, and professional bureaucrats all run the country. The party differentiation is mostly for show and marketing purposes so that one political party can gain more seats at the bribery table.

In practical terms this means additional jobs, money, and power in Washington for these political organizations. The winning political party and its members become wealthy and powerful in government by being bought and paid for through these firmly established and deeply entrenched bureaucracies in Washington.

The whole election process is simply about who gets to become wealthy and powerful via the bribery groups in this country. At heart, the elected officials represent the intermediaries in the trading process and are bribed so the entrenched special interest groups get what they want from the government. Meanwhile the American people are essentially the losers in this political game.

In summation, the American people and voters are being used by the Two-Party System and the decidedly broken political system collectively in this nation. I will address the American people directly, you are being taken advantage of, taken for granted, and in essence, you give credibility to this entire bastardized process by voting and participating in the patently unsound and thoroughly malfunctioning American political system itself.

The best course of action, most patriotic act that American voters could do to change this ineffectual political process and the broken status quo of the American Political System is by completely boycotting elections, stop giving any money to the political parties, avoid validating this cancerous and fragmented political process through active participation, and start demanding substantive changes being made to the failed American Political System as a necessary condition for future involvement.

The goal shouldn't be to elect better candidates, people, and politicians, it should be to change the American Political System itself! In other words, the current system can only produce corrupt and incompetent politicians, and a more effective and workable system is necessary to produce better candidates and elected officials for our government.

The American voters right now are essentially naïve and senseless sheep, they are stuck being mesmerized by the political herding dogs of the two dominant political parties. The American people are worked into a divisive political frenzy while the country as a whole is being sheared in the process.

Simply put, the American voters are a flock of thickheaded sheep, and the corrupt politicians are the sheepherders. If everyone abstained from voting, if all American voters as one unified front rejected the status quo of the failed American Political System, this would really send a message to the bureaucratic establishment and political ruling class that runs things in this country.

This is how you make a true difference; you stop accepting and acquiescing like a bunch of witless sheep to the status quo and demand real change in America. The system would have to change, otherwise you couldn't have legitimate democratic elections. The federal government would have to shut down until election buy-in was reestablished in order to validate government in the first place.

The American people and voters should stop being a herd of scatterbrained *Sheep* and cease participating in the charade of a political process until the system is changed. So the best way to demand change in Washington is to delegitimize the entire process. This means rejecting the political system itself as currently constructed in America.

But right now the entire American Political System is a sham cloaked in the forged guise of Democracy, and we have *the principle of Sheep* at the forefront of this broken political system, whereby the American voters falsely get their spurious self-identity through means of party affiliation and the Two-Party Political System, and this all needs to change.

The American people and voters need to wake up and stop behaving like a flock of mindless sheep, be patriotic and boycott the entire election process as an aligned and committed body which is not divisive but votes as a unified group for real change in Washington.

In discussing the general level of discord in this country, it is hard to ignore the prevailing trend of increasingly partisan divisiveness in America.[19] For instance, there aren't many landslide election outcomes these days, basically elections come down to which party can do the best job of motivating their respective political bases to get out and vote on election day.[20]

In assessing the big picture of American politics, there isn't a consistently strong political mandate on either side, with the Republicans getting support from traditional Republican states in the center of the country, and the Democrats getting support from traditional Democratic states located on both coasts of the country.[21]

In reality, there are a handful of swing states that frequently decide elections in combination with which political party does the better job of getting out the party vote during each election cycle.[22]

On the whole, voters are largely affected by this "Us" versus "Them" political mindset based upon which political party they worship at the partisan altar. These voters often talk past one another in the political debates that take place in America and rarely get past their own preconceptions and prejudices to understand different perspectives on issues.

---

[19] https://www.pewresearch.org/politics/2014/06/12/political-polarization-in-the-american-public/; https://www.pewresearch.org/fact-tank/2020/11/13/america-is-exceptional-in-the-nature-of-its-political-divide/
[20] https://www.aei.org/op-eds/presidents-seeking-reelection-in-a-land-without-landslides/; https://www.aljazeera.com/opinions/2020/11/5/the-landslide-that-wasnt-what-the-elections-say-about-america
[21] https://www.theatlantic.com/magazine/archive/2017/03/red-state-blue-city/513857/; https://en.wikipedia.org/wiki/Red_states_and_blue_states; https://en.wikipedia.org/wiki/2020_United_States_presidential_election
[22] https://en.wikipedia.org/wiki/Swing_state; https://www.history.com/news/swing-states-presidential-elections

In simple terms, most people have lost the ability to think critically about the individual issues facing this nation because they have been thoroughly brainwashed by the two political parties in our pseudo-democratic system like Scientology cult members. The American voters have limited ability to think rationally about politics, let alone make wise political choices as active participants in the manifestly flawed political system.

Issues like affordable medical care should be seen as American concerns, but these issues are framed by the political parties as partisan ideological subject matters. For instance, having affordable healthcare is either socialist, a communist ideology imported from Russia, or whatever marketing crusade will help condition Americans to vote according to the cultish political mandates of the Two-Party System.

However, this is all marketing propaganda, as no one believes or thinks that government sponsored roads and bridges are socialist or communist ideas. In fact, a lot of issues are framed, presented, and sold to the American people by the two political parties based upon what the business organizations, lobbying industries, and special interest groups who financially support the political parties want done in government.

This represents a major threat to clear and rational thinking on multifaceted issues, as these special interest groups ultimately influence the course of policymaking in America by contributing large sums of money to the given political parties which promote their various business agendas and ideological interests. For example, the NRA and the gun control issue, Insurance Companies and the healthcare issue, Teachers Unions and the education system, and Wall Street and financial market regulation.

Furthermore, I will posit that the country is so divisive right now, so brainwashed into this "Us" and "Them" political mindset that it doesn't matter which candidates run for elected office. In effect, these political candidates are all interchangeable, and elections are still going to fundamentally fall along the lines of the two political parties in the end.

This just illustrates the breadth and corrosive nature of the Two-Party System. These parties are essentially political monopolies that need to be broken up, as they have so much influence on shaping the vulnerable minds of voters, that voters have lost the ability to think independently and for themselves.

We basically have the Hatfields and McCoys phenomenon in this country that plays out in politics, as American voters are just conditioned to hate each other in an unthinking and highly visceral manner.

This endemic hate is so strong that American voters don't think logically and rationally about the specific issues. Moreover, just forget about Americans and the two political parties actually working together to solve difficult problems. This is no longer a democracy at work, but rather an internal "Bloods" versus "Crips" gang and turf warfare where both sides want to systematically destroy each other.

The goal is not to make the country better through political participation, but to defeat the mortal enemy in the other party like some bloodsport, with the ultimate party goal being to gain more seats in Congress, and thus more political power as a party. This is really a political civil war at the heart of this divisiveness, all spurred on by the two political parties like master puppeteers.

It is my contention in this book that this political divisiveness promoted by the Two-Party System is just not a good process, and the country as a whole suffers enormously as a result of this ineffectual state of affairs.

This divisive nature which is tearing apart this country is so acute and malignant that even if an issue or legislation would help the country, but it will make the other party look good politically, it will be opposed on principle alone. This underscores the reality that the political system is broken and needs to be changed. In short, political decisions are made based upon what is good for the party, and not what is good for the country.

It is not an exaggeration to point out that Republicans and Democrats exhibit the same signs and similarities of people in cults like Scientology and many of the organized religions. These members have become brainwashed partisan zombies that just regurgitate political party mantras and jejune phrases without thinking and logically examining the real underlying issues at the core of their political belief structures.

It is hard not to label political parties as religious cults these days. At heart, these issues should not belong to a single party, as they are American issues that are more important than the business of partisan politics.

There is also another dynamic which is in play here that is partly responsible for these cultish tendencies with political participants in our current system. In many instances, people have such unsatisfying lives in America that politics and being part of a team in the Two-Party System gives their lives a much-needed purpose.

Accordingly, you can bet that both political parties exploit this vulnerability in the American people for their benefit, and the overall prosperity of the party. In the final analysis, the Two-Party System is highly exploitative in nature.

When you factor in the dominance and power of the Two-

Party System in this country, its societal impact cannot be overstated, which is why we introduced the chapter going over this magnitude of political reach.

This political influence is so entrenched in the psyches of the American voters, from grassroots marketing activities in local communities all the way up to the national level, that the brainwashing and social conditioning is extremely hard to avoid and battle against as American citizens.

This is especially difficult for individuals who are highly susceptible and vulnerable to these types of persuasive behavioral conditioning techniques. And unfortunately, human beings seem to be natural followers from birth.

This probably has evolutionary value as a species, however, is detrimental towards rational and independent thinking on the individual level. Furthermore, this lack of independent and critical thought by individuals makes up a significant percentage of the American population and voters. This is precisely what makes cults and their behaviors, ideologies, and methods so successful and destructive for the human species and societies as a whole.

The American people and voters have an inescapable existential and spiritual crisis which yearns for a mental intervention from rationality itself, as they need to start working together as a group and find common ground on important issues facing this country. There are many difficult problems which require cooperation to address in a democratic system of government.

The whole idea behind a democracy relies upon the critical assumption that people will come together to solve these problems, that Americans will arrive at grand compromises which everyone can live with as a democratic society. However, this is impossible within the current divisive environment, which is promoted and defined by the Two-Party System in America.

It is obvious that the current political environment of far-reaching divisiveness is bad for the country, and the dual objectives of the Two-Party System will continue to divide Americans. This overarching purpose will never change, as it is good for the two political parties and their respective business models.

These political parties want division, and they sure don't want to work together in solving problems for the good of the nation. Therefore, the Two-Party Political System needs to be abolished, as the political incentives are entirely misaligned in this country.

It is time for a change or renaissance in politics and political philosophy in America. We need to abandon this "Us" against "Them" political mindset which so embodies the American political landscape today.

It is crucial that we find a path to change or significantly reduce the political divisiveness in the United States of America. As we are destroying ourselves from within, and our competitors are the ones directly benefiting from this highly dysfunctional and thoroughly divisive political state of affairs.

# 4 RACE & POLITICS

In this chapter we are going to discuss Race and how it is used as a manipulative tool in Politics to create divisiveness within society. When kids are playing together in the neighborhood no one is thinking about race. I lived in several ethnically and racially diverse neighborhoods as a child, and nobody made friends or played with other kids based upon their cultural backgrounds and physical characteristics. It just didn't matter to us at the time.

It is interesting that as people grow up into adults, develop as human beings, find career paths, and try to live their best possible lives, that they seem to care a whole lot more about race and ethnicity. Why is this the case?

Well, there are many variables involved in this dynamic, and I am not going to cover them all here, but one of the areas which definitely tries to separate Americans into racial categories is the world of Politics. The backdrop behind much of Politics is the fight over Power in a country, and the United States is no different in this regard. In a broader sense, much of life itself is a fight over Power.

It is clear that the world of Politics seeks to leverage the American people against each other, tries to fuel hostilities, create artificial conflicts, and in many cases exacerbate divisions among the American populace.

The prime culprit stands the Two-Party System in this country, as the more divided that Americans become, the better business is for the two dominant political parties that run the show in America. These two political parties really are the embodiment of evil when you get right down to it. They are both quite good at the business of not only causing but exacerbating hostilities and furthering divisiveness in America.

There are plenty of other American institutions such as the entertainment industry, advertising agencies, giant corporations, government bureaucracies, news media, and professional sports to name just some of the devilish culprits which also play an outsized role in separating Americans. These organizations love creating, categorizing, and dividing human beings into nice, neat little ethnic, racial, and social boxes like a bunch of branded cattle.

The American citizens are all being used as pawns by some organization or another, and there is usually the underlying motive connected with the pursuit of money and power as being the ultimate driver behind these manipulative activities, behaviors, and agendas. There is really no reason for Americans to hate each other because of ethnic backgrounds or have Race be this big of an issue in this country. In the final analysis, Race is big business in America.

It is ironic that in as little as twenty years with so many interracial couples and marriages, along with highly diverse populations in most major cities these days, that the laws of nature will make the whole notion of Race in America an archaic social construct. Moreover, it is going to be a tougher task to divide Americans by Race in creating artificial divisiveness for some end like Politics as the racial distinctions become murky at best and at worst are relegated to the graveyards of completely meaningless abstractions.

Here is one specific area that transcends the notion of race. This is the subject of human nature and sex which definitely transcends racial differences, as people have no problem being attracted to different ethnic backgrounds and racial categories, and subsequently acting out on these natural impulses. This trend in human nature even has evolutionary benefits as well.[23]

In this country both political parties are guilty of using Race and fears about racial and social differences to build political bases of voters. This is just flat out immoral, and why I call both political parties essentially evil, outdated, and unnecessary institutions. These two political institutions are just not healthy and positive contributors to society on the whole.

We have tried affirmative action as a practice, and it has done more damage than good in my opinion for the overall mental health of this country. It just results in another government sponsored program to classify individuals according to Race and create divisiveness within the American culture.

In fact, there should be no categories of ethnicity and race on employment applications, government sponsored Census Bureau modeling, and various other marketing databases, as they just wind up being used as segregationist tools in the end.

If we are going to fully move past the exceedingly limiting confines of Race in this country, and move on to the next, more

---

[23] https://aeon.co/essays/the-future-is-mixed-race-and-thats-a-good-thing-for-humanity

advanced stage of human evolution and societies, then we have to completely get beyond the notion of Race. And this ultimately means dropping the discussion of race altogether in society.

When Americans stop focusing on Race, we will be surprised to discover that there ends up being a lot less decisions, even in the areas of employment, government policies, and society as a whole being based upon racial differences. This will ultimately lead to more overall equality as a society and occur much faster than any other method of trying to artificially produce racial equality while simultaneously delivering competency and performance-based outcomes in America.

But once you embrace Race as a starting point, you have already lost the debate, exercise, and purpose of your original goal and endeavor. This is without fail, no matter how well intentioned. Even if the goal is framed from the outset as trying to lesson and eliminate racism in society.

The current approach in the country utilizes racial preferential practices to address racism, and the proponents of this strategy believe that the ends justify the means. However, this methodology is never going to achieve constructive and productive ends over the long term because it is based upon flawed foundations.

In fact, this methodology has underlying fundamentals which are both contradictory and nonsensical from a basic logic standpoint. Anytime you are picking winners and losers by means of racial preferential practices, you have gone down the slippery slope towards mediocrity, immorality, and societal ruin.

You don't cure poor race-based decision making with so-called better race-based decision making and maintain any credible and objective moral standard in the end. Simply put, you don't treat unsound practices with more unsound policies!

If you are using race as a determining factor, even under the guise of correcting past mistakes, you are further perpetuating the never-ending practice of race-based decision making. This exists at the core of what you are supposed to be fighting in the first place and is in stark conflict fundamentally with your own belief structures and overall moral philosophy. You have an illogical and invalid position which is highly contradictory in the end and makes one question either your intelligence or your motives.

When you think that you are helping equalize past racial injustices through racial quotas, certainly over the short term a case can be made that this is correct. However, only in the very limited micro view of this hypothesis, because over the long term you are doing far more damage when examined as an overall macro strategy.

This is for several reasons, but one of the many failings with this shortsighted approach is that you end up promoting what I refer to as this Fool's Gold Mindset which leads to the self-approving mentality that your work is done, "as we have hit our racial quotas."

This ends up being the classic case where you inevitably get precisely what you set for expectations at the outset. Put differently, one gets exactly what one tests for with regard to general outcomes and results.

Hence the net result with a truly colorblind society, whereby if you had no racial and ethnic quotas in the first place, you would end up with far more minorities in these same companies and government organizations over the long run by systematically eschewing the schizophrenic compulsion to utilize racial quotas as a basic social engineering strategy. Funny how that works isn't it!

Plus, you now avoid stigmatizing the racial and ethnic minorities in the process of your contrived social engineering experiment, as you blunderingly invited coworkers and professional colleagues to view these employees as quota hires.

The most damaging aspect of affirmative action as a social engineering ideal is that it opens the Pandora's box of doubting objective standards and qualifications. This is both internal to the candidates themselves benefiting from affirmative action, and externally from the outsiders to this wholly unnatural process.

This always opens up the lingering doubt that these socially engineered candidates were hired for reasons secondary to the fact that they were the most competent and qualified people for the positions. This is just too high a cost for any society to pay when examining the larger perspective ideals of always promoting the best and brightest regardless of physical characteristics and ethnic backgrounds.

In the final analysis, societies are actually much better off with the approach of never thinking about Race in any decision-making process, but rather humanity in general and societies specifically should strictly focus on the necessary skillsets and competencies of the individuals in searching for the best and brightest people to compete in a hypercompetitive world.

Once you start characterizing and thinking about people with regard to race and ethnic backgrounds as primary objectives, as opposed to their achievements, talents, intelligence, and overall competency levels, then you have failed as a society. We have indubitably failed miserably from this standpoint as a society.

The sooner that this country stops thinking in terms of race, but in terms of individual productive results, then the sooner we take that next step in evolutionary thinking as a species and an overall civilization.

When America stops discussing, thinking, practicing, and obsessing over Race, we will become really bad at the business of being racially motivated as a society. In other words, the more that you practice something, the better you get at this skill. If you are obsessively searching for Race Ghosts as a society, you are sure to find them lurking behind every corner.

We are pretty damn good at the practice of obsessing over Race in this country, as we socially condition our brains to think in terms of Race to such an enervating degree that our conceptual schemes have become thoroughly corrupted to the core. It is just unhealthy to think this much about Race, especially given the fact that America is one of the most racially diverse countries in the world.

It is obvious that America needs to deemphasize the subject of Race in just about all endeavors. This is because as soon as you bring Race into the discussion you have already lost the original purpose and lofty goals that you set out to achieve. In effect, you have poisoned the process itself!

In summation, forget about Race; instead, embrace and think Competence as a moral and political philosophy. There is a significant shortage of competency in our society today, and this applies to all races in this country.

There are just not a lot of competent people walking around society these days, and part of this is the result of the brainwashing propaganda of the American political system which has reduced many citizens to an analytically moribund state of politically unconscious zombiism.

In point of fact, many Americans just don't have the requisite ability to think critically about political issues given the sheer barrage of political propaganda they encounter throughout their lives in this dispiriting age of misinformation.

This country needs to think more logically. For example, we don't have racial quotas in the NBA, we just let the market work which dictates that the best talents and basketball skillsets must always prevail in the end. These natural market forces take precedence over any particular racial and ethnic backgrounds. Moreover, the market works quite effectively, as there are plenty of minority athletes represented in the game of basketball.

The same market forces also work in other sports like baseball, which sure doesn't have any racial quotas, and there is an abundance of ethnic and racial diversity in MLB. The same goes for many other sports such as football, soccer, track and field, and even horse racing.

The driving market force behind all these sports is performance, as there are objective standards which transcend ethnic and racial backgrounds. For instance, if a player can hit the curve ball, nobody cares which racial category this person checks on a government sponsored EEOC form.

This country has far too many Washington bureaucrats looking to create costly taxpayer solutions for problems which truly don't exist all things considered and are handled much better via the free market.

Another point to stress which demonstrates an interesting inverse relationship surrounding our meddling government policymaking is that we don't have government contracts in the NBA, we don't have government contracts in the music industry, and we don't have government contracts in the entertainment industry on the whole.

But yet, somehow these industries, all without the need for racial quotas are highly represented by racial and ethnic minorities, funny how that works, isn't it! Whereas academia, corporations, and government itself somehow needs and requires racially motivated quotas of all kinds for various political reasons in these industries.

I guess the real question here remains why there is such a strong correlation between racial quotas and government contracts. All of these institutions receive large amounts of money from the US Government in some form or another.

Hence, it appears that whenever the government is heavily involved with your particular industry, via handing out taxpayers' money, that racial politics is sure to follow. The US Government needs to let the Free Market work its magic and quit trying to intervene and micromanage market forces and outcomes.

It is quite apparent that we definitely go down a slippery slope in this country when we start believing that we need a certain representative racial makeup in every profession, role, position, and various institutions in our society. Just promote ideals and values around competency, achievement, effort, intelligence, skill, and creative energy and you will always be making good decisions based upon the right criteria.

Once you get in the game of defining outcomes based upon Race as a starting point, you are perpetuating the endless cycle of race-based discrimination. If we are going to be logically and morally consistent, discrimination of any kind is still discrimination. There aren't blessed discriminations, privileged discriminations or well-intentioned discriminations that are ever justified and morally acceptable in a Meritocracy.

Anytime you have discrimination and race-based decision

making, it is always wrong period, there are no exceptions. Somebody is always on the other side of racial quotas and being discriminated against because these decisions aren't being made in a vacuum and based solely upon merit.

Just ask the Asian students who are on the other end of race-based decision making with regard to getting into Ivy League institutions.[24] This blatant double standard has been so prevalent over the years that there are even terms referring to this systemic Asian quota within society such as the "bamboo ceiling" and "Asian penalty" pointing to the continuing cycle of race-based decision making which is clearly discrimination based upon Race as the starting point.[25]

Ironically, Asian students are minorities here in the United States, just not the right kind of minorities according to the political elites and the Ivy League institutions. Why is this the case? This is because Race has become so politicized and polarizing in America.

What we should have done in this country is acknowledged that all discrimination based upon Race is wrong, it is bad policy, and move forward as a society. Instead, what we did in America is acknowledge that discrimination is bad, and we are going to make up for this poor practice, by discriminating against other people based upon Race for all eternity.

This is a mistake which leads to the slippery slope we have today of pernicious unintended consequences whereby we are artificially creating divisiveness within society based exclusively upon Race, and it all starts with the helping hand of Politics.

Anytime there is this mindset centered around what are

_______________________

[24] https://www.cato.org/commentary/asian-american-ivy-league-applicants-can-trust-markets-more-courts
[25] https://en.wikipedia.org/wiki/Asian_quota

essentially inconsequential factors such as physical characteristics and cultural backgrounds which have nothing to do with competency, merit, and qualifications you have corrupted the process and lost your moral compass as a society.

Therefore, outcome-based decision making such as the following parochial political thinking is always wrong: "We need a certain number and percentage of racial and ethnic backgrounds in positions and organizations!" This mindset exacerbates and embodies the slippery slope slide as a society from a Meritocracy towards the Stygian abyss of Mediocrity.

Paradoxically, you have already defeated the whole virtuous purpose that you originally set out to accomplish. In a sense, you are sabotaging your original intent based upon a flawed methodology at the outset. This is even if the original endeavor and purpose is highly noble and has the best of intentions.

What is the perspicuously pellucid aphorism which reveals the fallacy with this line of thinking: "The road to hell is paved with good intentions!"[26] In the end, one must have sound methodology, if one expects sound results in reaching lofty goals as a meritocratic society.

It is interesting that prisons become bastions of racial segregation, where inmates join groups of similar backgrounds with race making up the primary category of division among the inmates in prisons around this country.[27] It seems that Race is the basest of human instincts regarding survivalism tendencies, and the political parties in this country exploit this

---

[26] https://en.wikipedia.org/wiki/The_road_to_hell_is_paved_with_good_int entions; https://www.samueljohnson.com/road.html

[27] https://en.wikipedia.org/wiki/Prison_gangs_in_the_United_States; https://theconversation.com/we-spoke-to-hundreds-of-prison-gang-members-heres-what-they-said-about-life-behind-bars-132573

basic survivalist predisposition connected with protection and the opportunity to flourish as human beings.

Effectively, these become crucial and important buttons to push in manipulating and motivating human beings into joining their particular political party as a form of political protection within society.

In a sense, the two political parties are similar to ethnic clans and gangs in prison, which are marketing themselves as political clubs or what I call political cults. Essentially, the Republican and Democratic parties are offering up and selling protection, survival, and the ultimate big lie of flourishing as Americans to their politically inebriated cult members via these highly effective and laser targeted marketing practices.

Again, any way you look at the problem, the two political parties in this country stoke much of the divisiveness that we see and experience in America. In reality, America has the same mentality as prison culture, and this is not a healthy, good, and productive outcome for a civilized society. Especially one that has a hard time working cooperatively together in solving difficult problems and achieving anywhere near its overall potential as a nation.

The ultimate irony remains that all these racial boundaries are going to become utterly blurred going forward anyway, and any distinctions that are made in this regard are purely arbitrary in nature.

These cultural, political, and social tools are meant to fundamentally manipulate and create further artificial divisions and hostilities within American society, and will only serve to lower overall competence, achievement, and future possibilities as a nation.

Therefore, the next time someone starts talking about Race

with regard to Politics, just stop them in their tracks, saying that you don't agree to those terms in the discussion. Politics should transcend Race, just like Sex, Love and Greatness.

John Mark Gray

# 5 POLITICS MAKES EVERYTHING WORSE

In this chapter we examine the nature of Politics itself, as in what does Politics mean, and how I am using the concept in this book. So there are many definitions in the English language for Politics. Let's get started with the following definition: "the art or science of government."[28] This quote is rather limiting in scope, and I would say that there is a whole lot more art than science in any discussion about politics.

However, I think it is inappropriate to put art and politics into the same sentence, let alone a broad discussion regarding the theory of government. It is just as important to nail down what you aren't referring to when discussing a subject, and this definition is sorely lacking for our purposes here in the book.

This next description of Politics gets us a little closer to some solid ground on the subject in the following: "political affairs or business, especially - competition between competing interest groups or individuals for power and leadership (as in a government)."[29]

---

[28] https://www.merriam-webster.com/dictionary/politics
[29] Ibid.

Now this definition approximates Politics in practical terms which we can relate to in our American form of government. I won't get into the debate here about whether America is a representative democracy, a direct democracy, or even a true democracy at all.

In real terms our government is a business, it may not have initially started out or was intended to be a business, but this is what our government has grown into, essentially a business enterprise.

Moreover, it is cutthroat competition by any means necessary to gain positional power which determines the course of our government's business ventures. It is this fight for power where Politics is used as the manipulating mechanism like a social sledgehammer to beat down the competition and separate the winners from the losers in our political system.

I understand why politicians use politics as a tool to gain power, to manipulate people and situations for their personal gain, as they are selling currency shares in their business. But why average American citizens often feel obligated to buy these same currency shares is beyond rationality itself, and one of the most destructive forces currently in American society.

In reality, American citizens need to exorcise their inner demons and get all aspects and notions of politics out of their personal and everyday lives. Furthermore, ordinary American citizens need to start holding their elected officials accountable and make them stop utilizing politics as a tool to manipulate the American voters in order to gain power in Washington.

As ultimately, the power in Washington gained through the use of politics as a manipulative tool is used by the politician not for the good of the country, but to enrich the business prospects of the career politician. The higher up you advance in the business of government, the more power you have, and the more money you make off of this power as a career politician.

This is why we need to change the business incentives in Washington by getting rid of the career politicians through various measures such as hard and substantive term limits. In short, the American government shouldn't be a business.

We need to get "politics" out of the governing process, and to accomplish this considerable goal, this means getting rid of the main culprit responsible for the promotion of politics within the political system, and this is the Two-Party System of Republicans and Democrats. Without this institution it will be much easier to get "politics" out of the governing process. As making everything worse is a common outcome whenever politics gets injected or introduced into the process or equation. The world is always better off without politics, period.

In fact, name me one thing, or think of one area that is better off with politics besides CNN's political advertising business during election season? In the current highly politicized environment, people care more about political outcomes than actually solving problems, getting things accomplished, and making things better in this country.

I argue that the introduction of politics into the cooking mix makes everything worse off as a result. It makes everything that much less enjoyable in direct proportion to the amount of "politics" inserted into the situation.

For example, the news recently that the ratings for the NBA finals were shockingly bad points to many problems with the sport, but I am sure the league committing marketing suicide sure didn't help sell their product to fans this year.[30] I realize we

---

[30] https://www.zerohedge.com/political/nba-finals-game-2-ratings-collapse-

live in a time where everyone dabbles in politics almost as a recreational hobby, but most things are much better without the interjection of politics.

As a matter of fact, I will go out on a limb here and say that Politics makes everything worse off, and I don't care if we are talking about business, science, music, sports, medicine, friendships or simply playing poker. These activities are all worse off when politics gets brought into the equation.

Unless your professional gig is actually in Politics, so you make money by virtue of politics, most people and organizations would be better served to leave politics out of their professional, social, marketing activities and relationships in this world.

This is actually marketing 101, as just strictly from a business standpoint, why would you want to alienate or offend any of your paying customers? This is a very competitive world where consumers have many choices these days, and no business can afford to alienate or offend their customer base or potential customers because of politics.

The major sports leagues have all gotten into this mode of being social justice warriors, and even the networks that cover sports like ESPN have interjected a large dose of political activism into their business strategy.[31] It is just a terrible marketing and overall business strategy in the final analysis.

For example, the people that agree with your politics, this has

---

68-all-time-low; https://www.zerohedge.com/markets/amidst-historic-ratings-plunge-nba-commissioner-says-league-likely-pull-black-lives-matter
[31] https://www.washingtonexaminer.com/red-alert-politics/espns-ratings-tank-due-skewed-liberal-agenda; https://society-reviews.com/2020/06/26/espn-goes-full-marxist-while-ratings-drop-to-all-time-lows/

the effect of you just preaching to the choir so to speak. It is the market segment that doesn't agree with your politics that you need to keep happy and satisfied with your product offering.

Moreover, the last time I checked, business franchises like ESPN, NFL, NBA, and MLB all need as many fans and viewers as possible to keep staying relevant and maintain a healthy fanbase which brings in the steady revenue streams.

Everyone enjoys the crazy money that comes along with the sports entertainment field at the highest level, well this all stems from advertising dollars, and advertisers are paying for large fanbases and healthy viewership demographics characterized by all political and social stripes.

These large multi-year advertising deals are not paying these enormous sums of money for professional sports leagues to become political activists and social justice warriors.

If truth be told, most fans want to escape the harsh realities of their everyday lives, and this includes the nasty political balderdash of the real world. These fans enjoy watching a sport or game of competition being played where they can watch sport for pure sport's sake.

The thing that makes sports special, is that great sports competition transcends race, politics, and social status. It is a place where people from different backgrounds, political viewpoints, philosophical and religious beliefs can find common ground in watching great competition and sport in all of its compelling, natural drama.

The true essence of sports is always made worse off by the interjection of politics, as are most things in this world. And it is quite evident that politics is destroying a lot of crafts and disciplines such as education, entertainment, law, medicine, science, technology and even art these days. In short, politics is making everything worse off, and most things in this world would be better off without politics.

Politics are not a necessary element for good sports drama, and when you are playing a game or participating in a sport, the last thing on your mind is politics. There are no fans watching the games and thinking to themselves, "you know what this game needs right now, is for one of the players to start discussing political theory!"

People don't seek out escorts for their views on string theory, and fans don't watch sports to learn about social and political justice. If these athletes really care so much about social and political issues, then switch careers and go become social workers or professional politicians.

But I can guarantee you that most fans don't give a rat's ass about professional athletes' political views. If they want to watch politics, they can just switch the channel to CNN or Fox News. In reality, athletes promoting politics are actually doing grass roots marketing for the business of politics, which effectively is promoting your competition with regard to viewership and attention such as CNN, Fox News, and the Two-Party Political System.

The real winner in everyone interjecting politics into their professional disciplines and careers is the Two-Party System of the Democratic and Republican parties. As a matter of fact, you are growing their respective political fanbases and viewership numbers, and essentially giving them more power and relevance over your lives as human beings.

I think everyone has been sucked into this political vortex of a black hole which only serves to give politics more power over their lives. In all honesty, franchises like ESPN and MTV would be better served focusing on providing high quality content and getting out of the business of politics. At this point it is rather clear that Politics is a thriving business, just not the business that you want to be in if your goal is to grow and maintain a healthy viewing audience over time.

Indeed, it really seems like ESPN and MTV are in a race over who can run their franchise into the ground the fastest. Both of these franchises are shadows of their former selves and have reached the stage of utter irrelevancy on the media landscape, as their ratings and viewership numbers point out rather clearly.[32] Spend less time telling me to vote and what cause I should support, and more time covering the essence of pure sport and bringing great music to my attention.

Just wait until the negotiations play out for the next television advertising deals, and I wouldn't be surprised if all the sports leagues are in for a rude awakening, as advertisers need healthy viewership demographics to sell products to consumers, and your job is to bring the fans, not turn off the fans with all the political drama they can get more than enough of on CNN and Fox News. This is a pretty basic economic and marketing principle to grasp for the professional sports leagues, simply follow the money.

Therefore, whenever politics starts creeping into the overall equation, specific endeavor or shared social environment, people in general and specifically participants themselves need to recognize it, and purposely make a concerted effort to change course.

Get the Politics out of the process and get back on course

---

[32] https://www.ibtimes.com/mtv-ratings-decline-raises-relevance-questions-young-people-cut-cable-cord-devices-1881468;
https://www.digitalmusicnews.com/2019/08/28/mtv-video-music-awards-all-time-ratings-low/

without the counterproductive nature of politics poisoning the environment. As it has a nasty habit today of serpentining into everything from advertisements selling products on television to the field of medicine, and even the once sacred paradigm of science itself.

The question is how to do this in real terms, and what are the practical solutions or steps to take in ensuring a politics free environment and cooperative workspace.

First of all, focus on the dynamics of actual problems themselves, make a concerted philosophical and methodological pact with each other as a society to consciously kick politics out of the discussion, and don't reward, hire, and enable politically motivated people. These political snakes are undoubtedly troublemakers, and bad for any endeavor, process, and social environment whether people realize it or not.

Secondly, use logic and reason to solve problems, put in the research and conduct your due diligence as an organization to determine what the actual objective evidence says regarding your activities and endeavors. Strive to take the emotional perspective and first blush reactionary approach out of the equation. It is also important to avoid doing naive, oversimplified cost-benefit analysis. And finally, infuse rationality into the problem solving and decision-making process as an overriding principle and fundamental practice.

Thirdly, hire people who are smart and capable of healthy, rational debate without getting emotionally attached and committed to ideological positions, especially when the evidence and a pragmatic solution demonstrating where it is possible to reach a grand compromise is available on these complex and difficult issues. In many cases, the pragmatic solution is staring everyone in the face, but people are so worked up by their ideological commitments that they cannot see the forest for the political trees obscuring their sense of rationality.

This paradigm shift is hard at first, but if you instill a politics free zone, people will start to view the corrosive nature of politics in sharp contrast with that represented by the new environment, and this ultimately results in people approaching problems with a more creative and open-minded conceptual framework.

This politics free zone or Anti-Politics Mindset brings people together as opposed to creating divisiveness and hardened barriers towards working collectively as a united team in addressing thorny issues and solving difficult problems.

Additionally, as time goes by it becomes easier to work as a productive problem solving team, as the stress and hostilities fall by the wayside and reverse the noxious effects of the stifling political environment where everyone is walking on intellectually and psychologically depraved eggshells, and similar to a butterfly leaving the cocoon, human beings can start maximizing their growth potential in this new renaissance era of the politics free paradigm where much harder social problems can finally be addressed and solved by humanity.

Politics blinds people intellectually, it stunts their overall growth as human beings, it narrows thinking options, and leads people to make bad choices. Simply put, politics makes people downright stupid when it comes to basic logic and reasoning abilities. This includes academics, business leaders, and professional politicians. In fact, politics makes everyone in society dumber than they would otherwise be as objective, rational thinking individuals.

In reality, we need Politics Free Zones in society, as opposed to politically motivated Safe Spaces on college campuses.

The main dilemma with thinking about Politics as a theoretical science is that in many cases Politics is not fundamentally trying to solve problems in the best possible manner or even on the basis of competent solutions from a practical applications standpoint.

In the current partisan environment, Politics has devolved into a purely agenda driven business enterprise, with the pursuit of control, influence, destroying the competition, group established hierarchies, money, and power being the primary underlying motivations determining political outcomes.

In point of fact, these political leaders aren't in hard pursuit of the truth. These politicians just want to win, push their partisan agenda, gain more unchecked power, and do the bidding of their financial backers whose own livelihood is often directly tied to a given political outcome.

Ultimately, this political outcome has been bought and paid for in Washington. This process is best characterized as political bribery, and one of the primary reasons for such bad policymaking on behalf of our government.

This remains what is wrong with our form of government and the overall political system, it is basically built upon the principle of bribery, pure and simple. The American political system is for sale, and everyone with considerable financial resources understands the game.

This leads to massive corruption and unrestrained bribery due to the pernicious financial gateway established via the two-party system, the corrupt lobbying industry, and the wrong type of individuals running for political office.

There is no other logically coherent way to think about the American political system at this point except for a severely broken and thoroughly corrupt system which greatly needs to be reformed in a substantive manner.

As a result, the entire Washington, D.C. bureaucracy from the Pentagon, CIA, FBI, K Street lobbyists, government lawyers, lifelong bureaucrats, and essentially everyone associated with the business of government in Washington for the last 30 years needs to be cleared out of these positions.

In point of fact, Washington, D.C., and our Federal Government has genuinely become a giant swamp of self-dealing and blatant corruption. The evidence is quite clear that Politics has effectively become a license for these individuals to conduct highly corrupt criminal enterprises in the course of doing business in the American political system.

Therefore, how do I define politics? Politics is the fight for power in this country, by any means, and by whatever methods necessary to attain this power. Thus, I get why politicians want to use politics as a tool to gain more power.

However, the average citizen who faithfully votes, seems to think that by supporting these leaders who they elect to political office, this magical process will somehow transfer or trickle down some of this power to them.

Furthermore, I could even see this as a logical argument and plausible political belief structure for voters originally, but after the last 70 years, or most people's lifetimes, and not even a morsel of legitimate power ever trickling down to ordinary citizens, one would think that they would completely reject politics as being in any way beneficial to their lives.

Yet this has failed to happen, human beings in general and specifically American voters, still not only embrace politics as important in their lives, but they fall for the same old political lies year after year, and election after election cycle in this country.

It is almost as if the American voters really enjoy being Sheep, that they would rather be slaughtered each election season, as opposed to rejecting the entire flawed process and broken system which has voraciously exploited them throughout their lifetimes in this so-called representative democracy.

There is little doubt that politics has made their lives worse, and a healthy dose of rational and logical reasoning makes everything better and might even be the Sheepherder's Achilles heel in the end.

# 6 THE BUSINESS OF POLITICS

I will open this chapter up with the following question: How much money is spent on politics over the course of an election cycle in this country? Just think about that concept, and how big this number is when you factor in all the people, groups and businesses who have their slimy little greedy hands in this American political pie.

Just to throw some numbers at you, the 2020 election spending is projected to come in around $14 billion, with congressional races making up $7 billion, and the presidential race coming in at $6.6 billion in spending.[33] There are over 2,000 super PACs which spent close to $2 billion in the 2020 election season.[34] The fact that there is an entire page dedicated to different kinds of political action committees on Wikipedia is symptomatic of what is wrong with the American political system.[35]

---

[33] https://www.cnbc.com/2020/10/28/2020-election-spending-to-hit-nearly-14-billion-a-record.html

[34] https://www.opensecrets.org/PACS/superpacs.php?cycle=2020

[35] https://en.wikipedia.org/wiki/Political_action_committee

The definition of a political action committee is the following: "a group formed (as by an industry or an issue-oriented organization) to raise and contribute money to the campaigns of candidates likely to advance the group's interests."[36] If you look at the top 20 PAC contributors in the 2019-20 time period, many of these groups are giving money to both political parties.[37]

It is obvious that these groups just want their interests taken care of in government, regardless of which party is in power or ends up winning the various election campaigns. If you don't think that this money buys considerable influence in government with regard to legislation and policymaking, then you need to seriously rethink this invalid position.

These groups and organizations are not giving all this money away without definite expectations that something will be given in return. Moreover, they have a history of such contributions through the years, so they know for sure that these types of campaign contributions pay substantial, tangible, and validated dividends for these business associations and special interest groups.

There is even a category called "Dark Money" for general campaign contributions, Leadership PACs, Foreign-Connected PACs, and Grants to Politically Active Nonprofits in this country.[38] As you can see there are no shortage of vehicles available for contributing money to various political candidates,

---

[36] https://www.merriam-webster.com/
[37] https://www.opensecrets.org/PACS/toppacs.php
[38] https://www.opensecrets.org/outsidespending/nonprof_summ.php; https://www.opensecrets.org/industries/contrib.php?cycle=2020&ind=q03; https://www.opensecrets.org/political-action-committees-pacs/foreign-connected-pacs/2020; https://www.opensecrets.org/outsidespending/nonprof_donors.php

campaigns and causes in this so-called representative democracy.

Furthermore, just like the tax evasion schemes on behalf of the major corporations in America, I am confident that all these big corporations and large special interest groups are well informed with regard to buying significant influence in the American political system.[39]

It is little wonder that things never change in this nation, irrespective of which party is in power in Washington, or who wins a given election cycle, as both political parties are positively bought and paid for by means of our corrupt political process.

Make no mistake, politics is a business, just like any other business in America. It is all about the money, and there is big money in politics. Like I always say, when in doubt, just follow the money trail to find out what is really going on behind the scenes in this world. Just ask yourselves, why is there so much money in politics? There have to be good business reasons for spending this much money on political campaigns during each election cycle.

I am arguing here that until you clean up the business of politics, i.e., get the big money out of politics, you are never going to clean up the corruption, dysfunction, and incompetence in Washington. Just look at how many people earn their living through the business of politics in this country.

This means there is a huge financial and monetary incentive to continue on with the corrupt, highly inefficient, and thoroughly broken political system. The continual promotion

---

[39] https://www.icrict.com/icrict-in-thenews/2019/1/23/how-big-tech-companies-avoid-taxes-and-what-can-be-done-about-it; https://fortune.com/2019/12/06/big-tech-taxes-google-facebook-amazon-apple-netflix-microsoft/

of this fractured status quo which is largely incompetent in most aspects of governing this country has eroded confidence in America itself.

When you factor in political advisors, consultants, lobbyists, polling firms, analytics companies, campaign staff, grassroots organizers, fundraising activities, and television advertising to mention just some of the commerce that revolves around the business of Politics. The parasitic nature of this political money grab becomes abundantly clear and predictably infinite in scope.

The list is rather endless regarding people and organizations built around the political ecosystem which personally benefit from the big business aspects of the American political system. It really shouldn't be a huge surprise why we have a corrupt government these days. It all starts with the fact that we haven't outlawed bribery in this country so long as it is couched under the surreptitious guise of political contributions and lobbying activities.

Just some of the questions that the American voters should ask themselves as passionate participants in this political charade that we call elections. Is there any good that comes out of this method of running election campaigns in the country? Does all this money buy better results or fairer outcomes for the American citizens?

Is this massive money spending extravaganza and the big business of campaigns actually good for a nation that thinks of itself as a representative democracy? Is this what the Framers of the Constitution had in mind when they envisioned the ideal form of government for the professed Land of Liberty?

This is what I mean by the fact that the American voters are Sheep, as just look at the dysfunctional political system underlying everything that is wrong with America. In truth, both sides of the political spectrum are complicit and guilty participants in the massive money paradigm and big business nature of the profoundly broken and thoroughly corrupt American political system.

It really doesn't matter who you voted for in the end, it matters who you bought and paid for in Washington. In reality, you have to be extremely wealthy, well connected politically, or part of a large political action committee to have your interests and issues addressed via the American political system.

Politics isn't about what is good for the country, but rather what is good for the party in power. The political party has business operations and primary objectives which take precedence over everything else with respect to governing. These include ensuring the promotion and stability of future political party jobs, wealth, and overall power.

The party that wins in these elections gets more of these political spoils. This is why the other party which maintains a minority status in Washington tries to deliberately sabotage the majority party in power and their legislative agenda. This makes it much more difficult to actually solve problems and get things accomplished in government.

Hence, if the majority party in power fails miserably, this is good for business because the minority party can leverage this failure to their advantage in the next election. This game theory strategy prevails for both political parties according to their primary goals in government, even if this means that the country as a whole and ordinary citizens suffer and are worse off as a consequence.

The only thing that matters for the minority party in Washington remains "sabotage politics" with the primary goal of gaining more power over the next election season. We saw this with the stimulus negotiations and the stimulus bill right before the 2020 election. Nancy Pelosi did not want Donald Trump and the Republican Party to get any possible political benefit from helping average Americans who were really struggling due to the Covid-19 shutdown of the economy.[40]

The Democrats in the House of Representatives were putting all kinds of special interest pork into the stimulus bill and were unwilling to negotiate or come together on a reasonable compromise to help ordinary Americans hurt by the fallout from the Covid-19 lockdown of the global economy. In fact, even some staunch Democrats thought this highly partisan behavior and politically motivated negotiating practice was inappropriate given the dire circumstances facing the American people during the pandemic.[41]

However, this isn't strictly a tactic of the Democratic Party, the Republican Party utilizes this same "sabotage politics" strategic tool to further their own future political aims for more power in forthcoming elections. This is all a game to these people, but the problem stands that average Americans regardless of party affiliation, always suffer the consequences of this sabotaging politics mentality in Washington by these political game players.

Consequently, any legislation that will help the country, but make one party look good is strategically blocked, stalled, and

---

[40] https://www.pncguam.com/pelosi-rejects-latest-trump-coronavirus-stimulus-relief-offer/

[41] https://www.foxnews.com/politics/democrats-pressure-pelosi-house-leadership-to-move-new-coronavirus-bill;
https://www.businessinsider.com/democrats-nancy-pelosi-white-house-trump-stimulus-offer-accept-republicans-2020-10

sabotaged in Congress. There is a long history of these deliberate sabotaging practices in Congress over the years, as both political parties utilize this tactic when the other side is in power. Ironically, even politics itself is worse off, when "politics" is introduced into the equation.

In reality, poor people and the average American citizen in the middle class is effectively left out of the political process. These people cannot afford to genuinely participate in the American political system, i.e., running for office because it costs so much money to finance political campaigns these days.

So just like in the business world, where the large companies absolutely crush the small businesses, the same goes for the American political system, big business interests prevail over the concerns and interests of ordinary American citizens.

Therefore, until you get the big business aspects out of the American political system, you have no hope for having fair and legitimate representation in Washington as an ordinary citizen who dutifully votes in elections each season, you literally are wasting your time.

The other aspect of this big institutional money in our political system, is the money wasted on politics that could be better spent in other areas like education, healthcare, legitimate infrastructure projects, cleaner cities, more parks, and an overall national commitment towards community revitalization efforts.

As most cities in this country are literally falling apart at the seams from a dearth of investment capital, and definitely lack the responsible planning projects for future development and growth necessary to meet the needs of an ever-increasing population.

For example, Michael Bloomberg basically tried to buy election outcomes in swing states like Florida right before the election in 2020.[42] How about getting the big money donors out of politics. This political campaign money would be better utilized as an investment in communities where it will truly make a social and humanitarian difference such as providing affordable housing, building better homeless living centers, and supporting drug counseling programs.

There should be a specific government tax category for the likes of George Soros, the Koch brothers, and Michael Bloomberg who historically are trying to buy political outcomes in America. We can call this the political corruption tax for clueless billionaires who obviously have too much money, significant political influence, and require much tougher campaign financing laws and regulations.

It has been established that whoever is in power in this country, irrespective of political party, we still get the same old results and overall sad state of affairs. It really doesn't matter if the president is republican, democrat, conservative, liberal, moderate, or even extremist in nature.

In the final analysis, it genuinely doesn't make a fundamental difference whether the president is a mean or nice person, a brilliant intellectual or absolutely dumb as a rock, we still get massive corruption, wasteful government spending, and forever and unnecessary wars.

The exact same problems still remain decade after decade as the politicians come and go in Washington throughout this never-ending cycle of massive political dysfunction and utter incompetence on behalf of a failing government.

---

[42] https://www.vox.com/2020/9/13/21434904/mike-bloomberg-100-million-biden-florida-2020-election;
https://www.cnbc.com/2020/11/04/bloomberg-sees-losses-after-spending-over-100-million-in-florida-ohio-texas.html

There is no positive correlation between voting and actually changing any of these stubborn and everlasting problems in America. We still have terribly bad roads, poor and decaying infrastructure, unaffordable healthcare, a substandard education system, rising costs, runaway inflation, reduced purchasing power, and an overall lower standard of living in America.

This obvious failure in government has definitely led to an all-around diminished quality of life for average Americans due to the massive fiscal mismanagement and incompetent legislative policymaking coming out of Washington over the last half century.

There is a reason that both parents have to work these days, even for upper middle-class families, as the overall standard of living versus the 1950s has been falling like a rock for decades in this country. The incompetent politicians of the last 70 years and the corrupt American political system are primarily responsible for the general decline of the middle class in America over this time period.

The American voters truly are Sheep if they believe voting makes any meaningful difference in this Nation. As everything is bought and paid for in this so-called representative democracy, and every single candidate who runs for elective office these days, regardless of political party is in it strictly for the money and power associated with this thriving business enterprise. The Business of Politics has religiously sold out the American people without a scintilla of hesitation, regret, and remorse.

These people wouldn't fight for political office if there wasn't a great deal of money and power involved in this business venture, and this results in precisely the wrong kind of people running for political office in America. And you think voting for one of these political grifters campaigning for elected office makes any difference?

In other words, if you start with a severely broken process, you inevitably are going to get seriously broken outcomes. This is always the case with any endeavor in life, and certainly reflects what is happening with the American political system.

Just take a look at CNN and Fox News and their ratings during the election cycle, consider how much money all of these political shows, online partisan websites, and supposed journalists make covering the Business of Politics.

In sum, everyone has their slimy, greedy little hands out along the political supply chain from giant corporations to large special interest groups all hoping to get some of this glorious money from the big business behemoth that is the American Federal Government.

Simply using a little bit of logical reasoning here, if Washington actually operated like a fair and responsible government without the deleterious effects and pernicious influences of big business, there would be nothing to see here, as there would be no material need for these people to be involved in the process because the United States Government wouldn't be for sale.

The very fact that all these people are involved in politics, suggests that not only is government a prosperous business enterprise when one gets right down to the heart of the matter, but it also signifies that government itself is an enormously corrupt, inefficient, and nonproductive entity in which influential outside parties truly believe beyond mere faith that they can surreptitiously manipulate to their own political ends.

Furthermore, this thriving business environment reinforces the case that the United States Government is unreservedly for sale to the highest bidder.

The logic is pretty straightforward here, otherwise, these influential outside parties wouldn't bother to squander all this time, energy, and resources manipulating the political process in America. Now one can clearly see that the incentives are misaligned in this country, and this is no accident.

Consequently, when you clean up the dirty money, take the business out of politics, and appropriately align good governing incentives, you inevitably clean up the poor practices in Washington. And who knows, when politics is no longer a business, then maybe voting will actually make a difference in this nation.

# 7 LOBBYING & CORRUPTION

There is little doubt that the lobbying industry in this country has considerable influence in Washington with regard to policymaking and overall legislation. And by the very nature of lobbying, this has corrupted the legislative and governing process, i.e., objectively good legislation independent of collusive influences and special interests doesn't actually exist in this presumed representative democracy.

But just how much lobbying are we talking about here in America? And just how pervasive are lobbying and consulting groups in this country? Moreover, what role and impact do they have on governmental policies? These are some reasonable questions to ask politicians at the moment when every single piece of legislation is filled with unrelated pork projects, onerous side deals, and contains poorly understood ramifications for the American people.

Well, the lobbying industry spent $3.4 billion in 2019, which was the most since 2010.[43] These are what some of the large corporations spent on lobbying for 2019 in the following: Facebook spent $16.7 million, Amazon spent $16.1 million, Boeing spent $13.8 million, Comcast spent $13.4 million, Northrop Grumman spent $13.3 million, Lockheed Martin spent $12.9 million, AT&T spent $12.8 million, United Technologies spent $12.7 million, Alphabet spent $12.4 million, and Southern spent $12.2 million.[44] These large corporations represent just the top ten on the list for 2019 lobbying expenditures, as the next ten companies on the list are also well known corporate names.[45]

These companies are not giving this money away to Washington for no good reason, as the practice reaps nice rewards. For instance, Adam Andrzejewski notes in the following Forbes article:

> Lobbying persuades and influences, and it works. The top ten Fortune 100 companies receiving the most federal funding saw an ROI on lobbying of 1,000 to 1. In other words, $1 invested in lobbying returned $1,000 in federal contracts and grants. These companies included Lockheed Martin, Boeing, McKesson, General Dynamics, Humana, Centene, United Technologies, Unitedhealth Group, Honeywell, and General Electric.[46]

---

[43] https://about.bgov.com/news/lobbying-spending-in-2019-reached-second-highest-point-of-decade/

[44] Ibid.

[45] Ibid.

[46] https://www.forbes.com/sites/adamandrzejewski/2019/05/14/how-the-fortune-100-turned-2-billion-in-lobbying-spend-into-400-billion-of-taxpayer-cash

In researching which industries spent the most on lobbying activities in the American political system from January 1998 through March 2020 we find the following: The Pharmaceutical and Health Products Industry spent $4.45 billion, The Insurance Industry spent $2.97 billion, The Electric Utilities Industry spent $2.56 billion, The Electronics Manufacturing and Equipment Industry spent $2.5 billion, Business Associations spent $2.45 billion, The Oil & Gas Industry spent $2.3 billion, The Miscellaneous Manufacturing and Distributing Industry spent $1.87 billion, The Hospitals and Nursing Homes Industry spent $1.79 billion, and The Education Industry spent $1.77 billion.[47]

Is it any real surprise that Americans pay more for medical drugs than similar countries around the world.[48] I am sure these lobbying practices aren't helping matters for US consumers who require these all-important medical products and healthcare services. In fact, there is a conspicuous positive correlation between the amount of lobbying activities and financial expenditures in Washington which is in perfect harmony with the ever-rising costs and fundamentally unaffordable nature of the healthcare system in America.

Additionally, I am rather confident that one could point to many other individual markets on the lobbying lists to similarly show how consumers and their interests are being rapaciously exploited by large corporations through these flagrantly

---

[47] https://www.investopedia.com/investing/which-industry-spends-most-lobbying-antm-so/; https://www.opensecrets.org/federal-lobbying/industries?cycle=a

[48] https://www.aha.org/news/headline/2019-09-23-report-us-drug-prices-far-exceed-average-11-similar-countries; https://www.drugwatch.com/featured/us-drug-prices-higher-vs-world/

destructive lobbying practices.

There are also foreign companies, governments, and special interest groups that are lobbying our policymakers in Washington. For example, the data reveals that 562 Foreign Principals have spent $2.37 billion since 2016 on lobbying activities in the United States.[49] And you wonder why certain countries receive preferential treatment in Washington regarding various foreign policy initiatives.[50]

If we banned all lobbying activities in this nation, including foreign lobbying activities, then this would eliminate these conflict-of-interest scenarios where motivations can be questioned on behalf of our policymakers and government officials. It is critical that foreign policy decisions be made from an objective and unbiased perspective, and not clouded by the murky world of financial lobbying interests.

In principle, there is very little practical difference between lobbying and record companies paying radio stations and personnel to play certain artists and songs which they represent, but somehow Congress doesn't see any similarities between this unacceptable business practice and their own participation in lobbying activities which absolutely brings into question their political motives regarding various policymaking decisions.[51]

---

[49] https://www.opensecrets.org/fara;
https://www.opensecrets.org/fara/registrants;
https://www.opensecrets.org/fara/foreign-principals
[50] https://www.cnn.com/2020/11/13/politics/kfile-douglas-macgregor-israel-lobby/index.html; https://www.timesofisrael.com/top-pentagon-advisor-said-pompeo-senior-officials-made-rich-by-israeli-lobby/;
https://www.nbcnews.com/news/world/pompeo-becomes-first-secretary-state-visit-israeli-settlement-n1248084
[51] https://globaljournalist.org/2019/05/pay-for-play-persists-in-music-industry/; https://www.rollingstone.com/music/music-features/pay-for-play-how-labels-pay-songs-radio-871457/; https://en.wikipedia.org/wiki/Payola

When lobbying is allowed as a basic political enterprise and thriving business practice in government, there are always going to be conflict of interest concerns which relentlessly threatens the very notion of democracy itself.

The obvious solution to these perceived conflict of interest concerns, would be to just eliminate any notion of impropriety altogether by banning lobbying completely. The fact that lobbying is wholeheartedly embraced and a thriving business model in government policymaking today, tells the general populace all they need to know regarding the political realization that there are a whole bunch of inappropriate behaviors taking place in Washington.

This corrosive political environment lends itself to harmful, poorly constructed legislative choices being made vis-à-vis the lobbying industry in this soi-disant representative democracy. Otherwise, just eliminate the practice altogether if high ethical standards play an important part in being a legitimate democracy.

However, right now there are too many corrupt career politicians getting wealthy off of this lobbying malfeasance like fat pigs gorging at the trough. In truth, America plays the role of a counterfeit representative democracy with purblindly pretentious patriotic passion like an unrepentant diva on the world stage.

The fact that there is even a street named K Street in Washington, D.C., that has become famous because of the multitude of lobbying firms, consulting businesses, and special interest groups taking up residence speaks volumes about the breadth, influence, and importance of the industry as a whole in

America.[52]

Hence, K Street in Washington, D.C., stands as a corrupt metaphor for the entire bureaucratic machinery dedicated to lobbying government officials on issues important to their powerful clients which include large corporations, foreign governments, NGOs, special interest groups, religious organizations, business associations, colleges and universities, hedge funds, private equity firms, and various other assorted parties. Not to mention the standard wealthy and influential billionaire seeking special favors from government these days.

I ask you, what is the fundamental difference between lobbying and bribery when you get right down to the essential and pragmatic details of the two practices? They both involve giving something of value, "Money" for certain prescribed and predefined outcomes or favorable treatment by those in powerful positions. In reality, these two practices are different in name only, and maybe one could argue, merely by the sophistication or nuanced style of the transaction itself.

But this is merely semantical interpretation and sophistic wordplay in the end, sort of like making fine distinctions between street hookers, prostitutes, professional escorts, massage parlor therapists, and outright gold diggers. It remains patently obvious what lobbying is designed for in this country.

The overriding purpose of lobbying is to provide a legally sanctioned means for wealthy clients to buy and influence policymaking in Washington. In effect, this lobbying activity represents a government sponsored criminal enterprise which

---

[52] https://en.wikipedia.org/wiki/K_Street_(Washington,_D.C.);
https://en.wikipedia.org/wiki/Lobbying;
https://www.opensecrets.org/federal-lobbying/top-lobbying-firms;
https://www.opensecrets.org/federal-lobbying/top-lobbyists

buys and sells corruption like stocks on the open market. This is all rather ironic and paradoxical when you think about it because true open markets don't exist anymore in America.

It is quite apparent that there is a significant conflict of interest problem going on in our political system. Therefore, it makes practical sense to legislate some constructive changes to the political process to address this obvious failing in government. In my mind, all lobbying needs to be banned completely in order to have purely independent and objective policy measures created and implemented which are good for the nation as a whole.

This of course is in stark contrast with the corrupt status quo which determines legislative policy based upon what is good for the lobbyists and their wealthy clients, as the deteriorating government debt picture reflects so perfectly in its sobering economic and political reality.

It's not like ordinary Americans can hire a lobbying group or have access to the expensive services of a consulting firm to actually participate in this purported representative democracy. Thus, this stands as unequal representation in Washington. Now you cannot still think that your vote truly means anything in these partisan dog and pony show ceremonial elections which unscrupulously sell Americans an endless stream of perpetual lies every election season.

In reality, just creating stronger or different lobbying rules, implementing stricter requirements, and having tighter regulations on these lobbying activities doesn't effectively work in curtailing the bad behaviors in Washington.

This is due to the fact that these are all half measures which doesn't address the insidious nature of lobbying itself, whereby forever leading to unacceptable conflicts of interest and wholesale corruption when it comes to fundamental government policymaking.

The sundry lobbying rules and regulations haven't worked in the past at any level of government, as these regulations just create various loopholes which are ultimately exploited by the smart and motivated lobbyists.

Moreover, the loopholes seem to be purposely created by politicians so that it appears government is cracking down on bad lobbying practices, but in truth, the loopholes end up being so big that the regulatory restraints have no material effect on the lobbying industry. The evidence speaks for itself on this matter.

Just look at how much money is spent on lobbying each year in America. These business associations, large corporations, and special interest groups wouldn't be spending all this money on lobbying if it didn't work and get the intended results.

There is too much of a historical record on the effectiveness of lobbying for these firms to just be guessing on the issue at this stage of the political game. They know by now whether lobbying works as a viable and effective influencing practice. So the inevitable takeaway here is that Washington politicians are for sale.

This is why so many former politicians who get kicked out of Washington political offices immediately get recruited by lobbying and consulting firms who leverage their vast political connections to gain influence in tailoring policy measures for the special interests and needs of their wealthy clients.

The regulatory oversight of the Lobbying Industry essentially requires an all or nothing approach, there should be no half measures in cleaning up these corrupt lobbying practices. Either ban the industry entirely or make the lobbying activities completely transparent and upfront to the general public. We can have full and open disclosure of the lobbying process by means of a public lobbying exchange.

This public lobbying exchange would consist of lobbyists putting these important lobbying issues on an open market exchange where the bidding would be public knowledge and out in the open for all Americans to witness firsthand. In addition, these lobbying deals should be presented in purely monetary terms, along with the names of lobbyists, financial sponsors, and legislators participating in the transactions on this real-time public exchange.

In this scenario, the politicians would have to publicly take the money for a given lobbying cause or conflict of interest issue. This out in the open approach would dramatically cut down on the corrupt and opaque dealings which occur in the shadows of government and are largely responsible for the expansion of these unethical lobbying practices in America. In fact, I bet this public lobbying exchange would go out of business faster than a politician can flip-flop on a hotly debated issue.

I am all for getting the lobbying right out in the open. These public lobbying exchanges would have the lobbying firm names, their clients, and funding sources visible for everyone to see, along with the associated deal prices in terms of financial commitments. In utilizing this transparent market exchange model, we could openly identify which politicians are bought and paid for by the lobbying industry.

My argument here stands that lobbying is a bad practice in principle, as it inevitably leads to corrupt politicians and overall poor policymaking in Washington. This country can no longer afford corrupt policy measures and special rules being written for wealthy clients, large corporations, and powerful special interest groups in Washington by our bought and paid for politicians.

It is quite apparent that allowing outright bribery, which is cloaked in euphemistic terms as lobbying activities, has very real negative consequences for the rest of the nation and its ordinary citizens.

It is very evident that many of the Big Tech firms in America have gotten away with a myriad of bad practices such as an outright censorship of content and speech that doesn't fit with their political views.[53] I firmly believe that these social media platforms are supposed to be objective, unbiased, and nonpolitical platforms.

For example, if they are favoring one political group over another, and they have monopolistic power, which many of these social platforms do exhibit, then they are arbitrarily and deliberately being used as instruments for suppressing the constitutional rights of Americans to have their political opinions and voices heard, i.e., free speech.

I am apolitical, so I have no ideological axe to grind here, and I find this behavior on behalf of the Big Tech companies rather disturbing as an American.

This is one of the most dangerous attacks on Freedom of Speech which has ever occurred in the history of this country. The fact that these firms felt empowered to even try this abhorrent practice speaks volumes about the immunity which

---

[53] https://www.economist.com/briefing/2020/10/22/social-medias-struggle-with-self-censorship; https://www.foxbusiness.com/technology/facebook-twitter-censorship-hunter-biden-report;
https://brownpoliticalreview.org/2020/03/its-time-to-hold-big-tech-accountable-for-political-censorship/

they felt their lobbying money bought them in Washington.

The takeaway here is that many of these Big Tech firms have become far too powerful and dominant in our society, and most likely need to be broken up for the good of the country. Alternatively, these firms need to be heavily regulated by government, a government that isn't receiving lobbying money from these firms to sway their judgment on the matter.

These firms shouldn't be in the business of censoring political views that they disagree with, that isn't their job, they aren't the political thought police. Moreover, because of their monopolistic power in society, they can have an outsized impact on the overall political process in this self-styled representative democracy. This dawning age of censorship sets a very dangerous precedent indeed for all Americans, irrespective of political affiliation.

What happens when these Big Tech firms disagree with some other aspect of how Americans should live their lives? This is a very dangerous precedent that has been allowed to stand in this once great nation that used to value Free Speech as a fundamental right.

Furthermore, I find it hardly coincidental that these Big Tech firms were all at the forefront regarding lobbying money spent in Washington over recent years.

It is also noteworthy that these Big Tech firms and their largely dogmatic and monopolistic practices have yet to be regulated by policymakers in the federal government despite an outpouring of complaints from consumers and ordinary citizens. I guess you can get away with a lot of bad behaviors and unethical practices in America provided that you have enough lobbying money to placate the corrupt legislators and spineless policymakers in our government.

Needless to say we require politicians in Washington who are not bought and paid for by the Big Tech monopolies who have wholly trampled upon the once sacred American value vis-à-vis Freedom of Speech and its primary role in preserving and protecting true democracy from the evils of tyranny.

This isn't just a Big Tech issue either, as many large corporations have been able to get away with similarly bad behaviors and unethical practices which are certainly detrimental and clearly unfavorable for consumers and ordinary citizens in this nation.

These consumers and ordinary citizens don't have the benefit of high paid lobbyists looking out for their interests on important issues such as Mergers and Acquisitions, Business Regulations, Corporate Taxes, and Labor Practices.

All these areas plus many others are subject to the pernicious influences which big money and the lobbying industry buys regularly with their sizable contributions in the American political system. It is patently obvious that lobbying has gotten way out of hand in America, and completely destroys any notion whatsoever of a legitimate representative democracy.

For example, let's look at the Military Industrial Complex and the lobbying component. We have many self-interested parties like Defense Contractors providing all kinds of financial resources to political campaigns and entrenched politicians who are highly supportive of military spending and enthusiastically dedicated towards promulgating and sponsoring these "forever wars" into sublime perpetuity.[54]

---

[54] https://maplight.org/story/defense-contractors-covering-more-than-half-of-u-s-with-corporate-pac-dollars/;
https://www.opensecrets.org/industries/indus.php?Ind=D;
https://www.opensecrets.org/industries/contrib.php?cycle=2020&ind=D;

This is all purposeful lobbying by these defense companies to make sure there remains continued support for significant military spending in Washington by the federal government. This "forever wars" mentality exists regardless of whether the country can actually afford this excessive military spending from a budgetary standpoint, which is certainly not the case right now according to our burgeoning national debt figures.[55]

Most of this expensive military spending and the large defense contracts are unnecessary and outright wasteful spending projects. These are essentially government sponsored corporate welfare programs disguised as patriotic spending initiatives which are not desperately needed to protect Americans from legitimate national security threats.

There is so much complete balderdash associated with the marketing of the military and the unwarranted and unequivocally wasteful spending which occurs for this budget category. This absolute mismanagement would almost be rip roaringly hilarious, if there weren't such serious budgetary ramifications and significant negative consequences stemming from this highly irresponsible and critically out of control military spending by our bunglingly inept federal government.[56]

In fact, most of these "forever wars" never solve anything except further the incessant agendas of the Military Industrial

---

https://www.opensecrets.org/industries/recips.php?cycle=2020&ind=D
[55] https://www.usdebtclock.org/; https://www.gao.gov/americas-fiscal-future; https://tradingeconomics.com/united-states/government-debt
[56] https://www.pgpf.org/blog/2020/05/the-united-states-spends-more-on-defense-than-the-next-10-countries-combined; https://www.nationalpriorities.org/blog/2019/07/18/us-spends-more-its-military-176-countries-combined/; https://www.cnbc.com/2019/11/20/us-spent-6point4-trillion-on-middle-east-wars-since-2001-study.html

Complex, and ultimately serve as specious justification for continuing down this tenebrous road of unchecked military spending. In reality these are government handouts via taxpayers to the large defense firms that lobby the heck out of Washington politicians.

This is the big business aspects of the military which continually talks their own book, finds a way to always spend and require more money, and never saw a war they didn't like!

The last truly necessary war was World War II, but somehow the American people have been sold war after endless war by the Military Industrial Complex. The Military Industrial Complex has never been held accountable by the politicians in Washington over the last 70 years in this nation.

It is this very state of affairs that Dwight D. Eisenhower, a five-star general in the Army, and the 34th president of the United States, warned this country about regarding the dangerous potential for abuses of power by the Military Industrial Complex.

This worry by Eisenhower is eloquently stated in the following excerpt from his famous farewell address to the nation:

> In the councils of government, we must guard against the acquisition of unwarranted influence, whether sought or unsought, by the military-industrial complex. The potential for the disastrous rise of misplaced power exists and will persist. We must never let the weight of this combination endanger our liberties or democratic processes. We should take nothing for granted. Only an alert and knowledgeable citizenry can compel the proper meshing of the huge industrial and military machinery

of defense with our peaceful methods and goals, so that security and liberty may prosper together.[57]

The whole reason for these "forever wars" that waste precious time, resources, and ultimately lives is to justify ridiculously out of control military spending in the first place, and you can bet that lobbying is heavily used as the motivational tool in helping facilitate this entire broken and corrupt process vis-à-vis the American political system.

The decisions to pursue military objectives often have a large conflict of interest component inherent in them, and far too often we are left with the fox guarding the hen house in regard to military spending and lucrative defense contracts. This represents money which is being poorly spent and wholly mismanaged by our federal government.

These are taxpayer dollars that could be better spent in other much-needed areas such as investing towards providing affordable healthcare coverage for all Americans and improving our lagging education system which is plainly failing in the highly competitive global marketplace.

There exists another concerning issue with regard to the lobbying industry in this country. It is the fact that the lobbyists are the ones effectively writing these bills in Washington. You don't honestly believe that any of these idiots in Congress are smart enough to write word one in a bill themselves about a particular industry.

These legislative bills are written by industry lawyers and

---

[57] https://avalon.law.yale.edu/20th_century/eisenhower001.asp; https://en.wikipedia.org/wiki/Military%E2%80%93industrial_complex; https://www.c-span.org/video/?15026-1/president-dwight-eisenhower-farewell-address

professional lobbyists who make certain they get all their necessary goodies included in the legislative bills. These highly compensated bureaucrats, lawyers, and lobbyists make sure to include items which are beneficial to the special interest groups they represent in Washington, often at the hefty expense of ordinary citizens.

For example, the Big Tech firms have considerable influence in writing the language for regulatory bills relevant to their industry. Likewise, Wall Street has significant impact in dictating the terms regarding financial market legislation and overall regulation.[58]

How do you think the 2007-08 financial crisis happened in the first place? Wall Street lobbied heavily for the very instruments of high leverage derivatives that helped create the 2007-08 financial crisis in America.[59]

In fact, Hank Paulson both lobbied for more leverage on behalf of Goldman Sachs, and then turned right around and served as the Treasury Secretary in an oversight function, to clean up the very mess which this increased leverage played in the absolute implosion of investment banks on Wall Street during the 2007-08 financial crisis.[60]

Indeed, talk about the proverbial fox guarding the henhouse,

---

[58] https://hbr.org/2014/06/the-price-of-wall-streets-power
[59] https://www.thebalance.com/what-caused-2008-global-financial-crisis-3306176; https://www.reutersevents.com/sustainability/business-strategy/what-role-did-lobbyists-play-financial-meltdown; https://en.wikipedia.org/wiki/Inside_Job_(2010_film)
[60] https://www.propublica.org/article/top-regulators-once-opposed-regulation-of-derivatives; https://www.sourcewatch.org/index.php/Goldman_Sachs; https://en.wikipedia.org/wiki/Net_capital_rule; https://www.investopedia.com/articles/economics/09/financial-crisis-review.asp

this serves as another prime example of what is terribly wrong with the American political system.

There is also ample evidence that the large drug and health insurance companies, along with other major healthcare and medical industry players had considerable influence and input into the formulation of the Affordable Care Act also known as Obamacare.[61]

No wonder a majority of the healthcare firms and pharmaceutical companies didn't go out of business after the passing of the Affordable Care Act, as a really good healthcare bill would have put many of these companies out of business for good.

The Green NGOs and the Environmental Industry heavily lobby politicians in Washington concerning what is included in environmental and energy legislation. The same goes for other interested industries such as Construction, Oil & Gas, and Transportation in this alleged representative democracy.

In other words, every single major industry in America is bribing politicians in Washington for special treatment vis-à-vis government policymaking. Meanwhile, the average American citizen has no input or say regarding what goes into these legislative bills. And you still think your vote impacts anything that happens with respect to the business-as-usual political climate in Washington? I have news for you, it doesn't.

It shouldn't come as a giant surprise that every single major industry gets their powerful tentacles into these legislative bills

---

[61] https://www.theguardian.com/commentisfree/2012/dec/05/obamacare-fowler-lobbyist-industry1;
https://www.npr.org/templates/story/story.php?storyId=125170643;
https://publicintegrity.org/health/lobbyists-swarm-capitol-to-influence-health-reform/

in Washington. This explains why average consumers and ordinary citizens are constantly being punished by government policymaking in the course of subsidizing large corporations and special interest groups above everything else in America.

The average American has no political clout where it counts because lobbying requires large amounts of money to have a legitimate seat at the influencing table. Lobbying makes America a rigged game which nullifies the power of voting to enact real change in the government bureaucracy. In many cases, members of congress are besieged with more lobbyists working on influencing their positions regarding legislative bills than these people have congressional staffers.

These deep-rooted bureaucrats, lobbyists, and special interest groups are effectively the ones who are running the show in Washington. As a standard operating practice, these lobbyists put little ancillary items and sneaky unrelated matters into legislative bills like Christmas stocking surprises that cost taxpayers dearly in terms of unsustainable debt obligations down the line. This behind-the-scenes activity represents extra pork which has absolutely nothing to do with the original bills being written in congress.

For instance, the Unlawful Internet Gambling Enforcement Act (UIGEA) of 2006 was slipped into the SAFE Port Act at the last moment, and many believe that special interest groups played a significant role in this legislative sleight of hand.[62]

Do you honestly believe that online poker has anything

---

[62] https://en.wikipedia.org/wiki/Online_poker; https://en.wikipedia.org/wiki/Unlawful_Internet_Gambling_Enforcement_Act_of_2006; https://en.wikipedia.org/wiki/United_States_v._Scheinberg; https://www.laweekly.com/black-friday-how-the-feds-shut-down-online-poker/

remotely to do with port security in this country? These are the kinds of legislative shenanigans that routinely take place in Washington. In fact, these legislative backroom deals which have transpired for decades in congress need to be prevented because they always have a major conflict of interest component lurking nearby.

I continue to believe that an absolute and complete ban regarding all lobbying activities would definitely be a meaningful step in the right direction for reducing overall corruption within our government policymaking.

The fact that politics runs through the middle of farmland country via the Iowa caucuses every two years for both the midterm and presidential election seasons has significant political costs associated with this course of events.

This gives extra influence and overall power to the Agriculture Industry and their lobbying arm in Washington, and you can bet that this influence provides considerable sway regarding the creation of special benefits and preferential treatment for farmers and the agricultural business in this illusive representative democracy.[63]

The misalignment of incentives with regard to the Agriculture Industry, and the poor legislation written in Washington that we call farm bills in this increasingly diminishing and failing free market economy is a complete abomination of sound policymaking.

------

[63] https://en.wikipedia.org/wiki/Iowa_caucuses;
https://en.wikipedia.org/wiki/Elections_in_Iowa;
https://www.downsizinggovernment.org/agriculture/subsidies;
https://www.nal.usda.gov/topics/agricultural-subsidies;
https://www.taxpayer.net/agriculture/usda-farm-subsidies-at-highest-level-in-20-years/

This political ineptitude didn't happen in a vacuum, and the lobbying industry is directly at the center of this legislative mismanagement of agriculture by congress through the years.

But this should come as no great surprise to Americans, as almost every business or industry which is strong and wealthy enough to afford a powerful lobbying group to represent their interests in Washington, ends up determining our government policy for said business or industry without fail. This is truly what it means to be a representative democracy today, it just requires extremely deep pockets to buy this elusive representation in government.

This is bribery pure and simple, the unprincipled political practice is just spun and marketed euphemistically as lobbying and information gathering for the benefit of policymakers in Washington. No wonder these legislative bills are so poorly written in this nation.

America has become a thoroughly corrupt country where everything is for sale to the highest bidder, all under the bureaucratic guise of the uncompromisingly legal, yet wholly unethical practice of government sanctioned lobbying activities.

Remember when Nancy Pelosi said back in 2010, "We have to pass the bill so that you can find out what is in it."[64] This was actually a form of Freudian slip on her part, as what she really subconsciously revealed in this statement is the underlying notion that congress often doesn't know what is in these legislative bills.

I would lay good odds that most members of congress have very little firsthand knowledge regarding the substantive details

---

[64] https://www.usnews.com/opinion/blogs/peter-roff/2010/03/09/pelosi-pass-health-reform-so-you-can-find-out-whats-in-it; https://www.youtube.com/watch?v=9uC4bXmcUvw

of the legislative bills that they are voting on at the time.

The historical evidence is quite clear in this respect, the members of congress are led around by their respective noses via the lobbying and special interest groups, and this insidious financial habit is negatively affecting most of these political issues which are legislated in Washington.

In good truth, I think the more accurate statement would be that members of congress will know what is in these legislative bills when their congressional minions actually read the bills that are effectively written by the unscrupulous industry lawyers and lobbyists.

And only then, when the congressional staffers have gone over the substantive details of these legislative bills will someone in our cumbersomely bureaucratic government be well enough informed to finally educate the incompetent members of congress as to what is really in these atrocious bills.

After all, the members of congress have to eventually explain or market this legislative action back home in their respective congressional districts. In other words, the thoroughly corrupt politicians need to justify these terrible legislative bills to their gullible constituents, so they better formulate a convincingly good story full of half-truths and outright lies.

This is what happens when you elect a bunch of bovinely stupid and thoroughly untalented political hacks who are not capable and competent enough to actually write their own legislative bills in congress. These inept politicians couldn't write their own legislative bills even if their very lives depended upon it.

When I was a kid, there were these comically entertaining Saturday morning cartoon spots trying to educate kids about how bills become laws. Of course, these amusingly naïve political cartoons conveniently left out the corrupt lobbying activities in the discussion, which ultimately are best characterized as bribery practices in the end.

You cannot have a true democracy when you utilize bribery as a state sponsored enterprise to enact the laws of a nation and expect the citizens to meaningfully obey these corrupt laws such that they were legitimate in the first place.

Lobbying is a corrupt activity when you get right down to it, it significantly compromises the integrity of the political system, and needs to be banned altogether as a government practice in this country.

Until legalized bribery is prohibited, expect this surreptitious business-as-usual mentality and incestuous continuation of bad policies created by the lobbying industry like the aforementioned UIGEA piece of legislative brilliance, all with the express intent of subverting the democratic process in Washington via the corrupt career politicians, entrenched piggish bureaucrats, and powerful special interest groups which are truly running our government into apocalyptic ruin.

# 8 VOTING DOESN'T MATTER

One of the major themes in this book is that voting doesn't really matter in the end. This dovetails nicely with another major theme of the book which is that not voting or abstaining from any participation in the voting process does in fact matter and will genuinely make a substantive difference by ultimately demanding accountability in this once great nation.

I am basically turning the problem upside down and putting the very act of political participation on its head. Instead of voting and making a difference, what if we did the exact opposite as a country? What do Americans really have to lose at this point by not voting? It simply isn't the case that voting over the last 70 years has made any meaningful and positive change in the overall governance of America.

In fact, the country is losing prominence on the world stage, problems keep getting bigger every year, and Americans on average are worse off from an economic standpoint when you analyze key factors such as living standards, purchasing power, and overall quality of life.

The argument goes that instead of voting, the most impact which Americans could have in making meaningful change in Washington is actually by not participating in the broken and corrupt political process. In essence, the voters are refusing to legitimize the status quo that obviously isn't working and are demanding real fundamental changes be made to the political system by means of this strategic approach.

I will reiterate the point, what do the American voters have to lose at this juncture by sitting out as an organized block that makes known the idea that the political system is broken, and they are demanding real change from government and policymaking in Washington.

It just isn't the case that things are going to get better or real change will happen in Washington by voting, and this remains a political truism regardless of which party is in power. Thus, object to the entire notion that voting makes a difference, because take a hard look at our nation, voting doesn't make a significant difference, and hasn't for the last 70 years of poor governance on behalf of both political parties.

What will really make a difference is if everyone stays home and refuses to vote as a unified body of political contempt for the failed system of government which has absolutely lost its moral compass.

This is crucial, you need large numbers for the political boycott to work, it needs to be highly organized, and people have to be resolutely disciplined in staying away from the corrosive voting ecosystem altogether.

The bigger this political rejection movement becomes, and the more voters who stay home, the greater impact this approach has on ultimately bringing about substantive change to the unrepresentative governing process and thoroughly corrupt system that is utterly failing most Americans right now.

All these people in Washington respect power, and a massive voting block which stays home and rejects the entire sham of a political process, garners a lot of power. The reasoning here is that everyone in Washington loses their jobs if the country shuts down with a full-fledged political revolution. And ultimately, the numbers decide if the revolution has any real legitimacy as a political movement.

In a realistic sense, politicians are the most susceptible to going whichever direction has the primary momentum and the latest support. Oftentimes, these spineless government leeches have no real intellectual or leadership views of their own independent of which way the political winds are blowing on that particular day.

However, if more people who normally vote all abstain from participating in the voting process, so the effect is that there are far more non-voters compared to participating voters, this questions the entire legitimacy of the status quo, and real changes will have to be made to the political process and government system as a whole.

Otherwise, the next step is continuing on with a thorough repudiation of the American political system via an American revolution. Hence, the *Stop the Vote* campaign only works if large numbers of American citizens join the movement.

But we should not underestimate the strategic approach where everyone stays home and refuses to vote as a unified and committed body of righteous political objectors. This serves the truly patriotic purpose of declaring political war against the entrenched and established zealously partisan ruling class in this nation which has been incompetently running the show in Washington for decades.

This movement is showing through abstention that they are no longer going to foolishly support the incompetent status quo of partisan politics in Washington and the thoroughly corrupt business as usual destructive policies that are ruining this country. It is definitely time for an American political revolution.

So what would it take to motivate voters to stay home in large numbers, enough to actually incentivize the political ruling class and avowed democratic system to take notice and make the necessary changes to appease this righteous group of political strikers?

Just to ground the discussion in some numbers right here. The turnout for the Voting Age Population (VAP) as a percentage is roughly 55 percent and the Voting Eligible Population (VEP) as a percentage is approximately 60 percent for presidential elections in America.[65]

Simply put, think in terms of (VEP) as registered voters, and (VAP) representing residents in the nation who are 18 years of age and older, and this metric parenthetically includes nonregistered voters, noncitizens, and convicted felons depending upon the state.[66]

Of course, the numbers are lower for midterm elections with these two voting participation metrics falling roughly in a range between 40 and 50 percent depending upon the data source and

---

[65]

https://en.wikipedia.org/wiki/Voter_turnout_in_United_States_presidential_elections; https://www.presidency.ucsb.edu/statistics/data/voter-turnout-in-presidential-elections

[66] http://www.differencebetween.net/miscellaneous/politics/difference-between-vep-and-vap/; https://felonvoting.procon.org/state-felon-voting-laws/

the given election year.[67]

It is important to take all these numbers with a large grain of salt, as the United States has very poor government data records for almost every sector of the economy and our overall reporting methodologies as a whole are tremendously flawed.[68]

The important takeaway is that many Americans have already given up hope on the idea that voting makes a real difference in the bigger picture of this giant government bureaucracy which continues to grow unabated and is relentlessly more intrusive upon our everyday lives regardless of which political party is in power.[69]

It is also noteworthy that we have had some rather dismal voter participation rates which have dropped down into the upper 30 percent range for midterm elections, and the lower 50 percent area for presidential elections, and it is still business as usual with the partisan ruling class in Washington.[70]

In other words, for any voting participation boycott to fundamentally work, it has to be rather large in scale to get politicians to pay serious attention to the American citizenry. For instance, these participation metrics will have to fall into the 20 percent range for midterms and the 30 percent area for presidential elections to effectively shock the political ruling class to start acting responsibly and actually being accountable

---

[67] http://www.electproject.org/home/voter-turnout/voter-turnout-data; https://www.npr.org/2018/11/08/665197690/a-boatload-of-ballots-midterm-voter-turnout-hit-50-year-high; https://www.census.gov/content/dam/Census/library/stories/2019/04/behind-2018-united-states-midterm-election-turnout-figure-1.jpg

[68] https://www.census.gov/topics/public-sector/voting.html

[69] https://www.pewresearch.org/fact-tank/2020/11/03/in-past-elections-u-s-trailed-most-developed-countries-in-voter-turnout/

[70] https://www.statista.com/statistics/1139251/voter-turnout-in-us-presidential-and-midterm-elections/

to the American citizens once again.

In truth, for this movement to work you need to put legitimate fear into the professional politicians! These political grifters have to understand that the American people are no longer going to enable their bad behaviors and poor performance in leadership positions which are unquestionably ruining this nation. In summation, the American people need to rise up and stop behaving like a rather docile flock of Sheep.

It is time for the American people to truly band together and demand real change from our government. The first step is someone starting an organization, a movement if you will, that gains traction in the minds of the American people and eligible voters.

This means that there will have to be a leader of the movement, and this leader will need to be good at communicating what the political movement stands for from a values standpoint. This nonpartisan leader will have to earn credibility with the American people through objectively good words and actions.

It will be critical to convey rather clearly what the movement is trying to accomplish regarding making substantive changes to the broken political status quo which is failing most Americans right now.

Moreover, the American people have to buy what the movement is selling, as all ideas involve selling and marketing, even if they are objectively good, logically valid, and meaningful ideas in the end.

Inevitably, every burgeoning political paradigm starts with the marketing of new ideas.

Ultimately, the American people have to want change, and believe that this strategy is a good way of bringing about and making major changes in our political system. The collective will of the American people for real change in government remains an open question right now.

Maybe the American people don't want to make any substantive changes, as perhaps these are too extreme measures in their minds, and perchance the American voters are happy with the broken status quo of our current political system. The old saying, that you can lead a horse to water, but you can't make it drink applies here.

I have witnessed this maxim and principle play out many times in life, as most human beings would rather keep doing what they want to do, even if the solution in solving their problems is presented to them on a silver platter.

It may just be that human beings are destined to always be *Sheep*, and the world is right in balance if they are being used and taken advantage of by their political leaders.

But let's say that people can rise up and stop being Sheep. An effective organization with an incorruptible purpose, which reaches large enough numbers to constitute a sound majority, possesses enough power to make substantial changes in this country, and upsets the status quo of the perpetual ruling class in Washington would definitely be a worthwhile cause.

Obviously, size is the entire key to the political change equation here, as the bigger the movement, the more realized power the movement has to affect change in this country. In reality, a movement which gains political strength and holds great magnitude such that it could demand legitimate political change will have sufficient financial power through its sheer size alone.

And as I always say, never underestimate the power of money in affecting change in this nation. So obviously the wealthy and deeply entrenched political class in this faux representative democracy are going to use their vast resources to try and block this American political revolution, but an organized, ideologically unified, and highly committed movement which reaches majority size surpasses all monetary considerations in the end.

I will just say this, that it will take quite a charismatic leader to bring enough Americans together from the different socially, politically, and ideologically conditioned backgrounds of the Two-Party System to essentially cross partisan lines and join forces in a unified and coherent patriotic movement which successfully takes back this country from the corrupt and incompetent career politicians that have thoroughly bankrupt and destroyed America.

We are talking the likes of a Martin Luther type of individual that could take on the power structure of the massive Catholic Church in the Protestant Reformation, this is what monumental task faces the American citizens these days.[71]

In principle, America needs not a Protestant Revolution, but a full-fledged American Revolution. However, the historic significance of the Protestant Revolution on all of Europe and not just the Catholic Church is quite an apt comparison to be made here.

An organized movement which brings about real change in this nation, one that brings people together across divisive partisan lines, will constitute a real paradigm shift in America.

Furthermore, the ramifications of this American Revolution will not only change government as we know it today, but will

---

[71] https://en.wikipedia.org/wiki/Martin_Luther;
https://en.wikipedia.org/wiki/Reformation;
https://www.history.com/topics/reformation/reformation

reverberate throughout the entire world, and inspire others to rise up against corrupt and incompetent governments.

Usually for this type of dramatic change to occur in societies, things have to get really bad in the country. However, I have been surprised by how long Venezuelans have put up with their broken government state and series of incompetent leaders, especially over the last decade with rampant inflation, severe food shortages, rising crime, and overall deteriorating conditions in the country.[72]

Therefore, it seems there are multiple factors that go into any meaningful political revolution equation.

In the abstract, one can definitely imagine a state of affairs where things get so bad in this nation that this paves the way for a dramatic paradigm shift in political thought.

Although the abstract is becoming increasingly concrete in the winds of change, as the current rapid descension into absolute government tyranny continues unchecked, the American people may be pragmatically approaching the hauntingly familiar revolutionary horizon that awakens the democratic spirit of true patriotism once again, and are rationally moving towards the distinct possibility of embracing more extreme measures to force legitimate, significant, and world-shattering changes upon their failing political system.

These massive paradigm shifts with regard to metamorphic political revolutions don't occur that regularly in society in terms of people's lifetimes, every three hundred years or so on average when you look back through the history and evolution

---

[72] https://en.wikipedia.org/wiki/Hyperinflation_in_Venezuela; https://en.wikipedia.org/wiki/Shortages_in_Venezuela; https://en.wikipedia.org/wiki/Crime_in_Venezuela; https://en.wikipedia.org/wiki/Crisis_in_Venezuela

of humanity.

So this is the magnitude of seismic change that will be required to bring about competent and responsible government policymaking, a systematic reduction in the high levels of bureaucratic corruption, and to significantly improve things altogether in the American political system.

I have not underestimated the significance of this event, as this requires a profound change in the way Americans think about politics, our government, and the political process. This is why I put a rather low probability on this type of monumental paradigm shift in political thought occurring during my lifetime.

The more probable outcome is that smaller changes and slight adjustments get incorporated into the political system on the margins. This is why I lay out different levels of potential political changes that can be made to the American political system which improves the overall functioning of the system and makes it operate in varying degrees better.

I am a pragmatically practical person in the end. I am individually willing to commit to a full-fledged American revolution, however, I am just not sure the American people are ready to make this same kind of commitment from a politics standpoint.

If we take stock of where we are currently as a country, the American voters are thoroughly brainwashed by the propaganda machinery of the two-party system, a complicit and immoral news media, and the steadfastly vacuous American cultural institutions like Hollywood, Apple, and Celebrity Influencers.

The malefic effects of this cultural brainwashing are similar to those of zombified cult members who are rationally hijacked by Scientology.

In point of fact, the American voters are moronically stupid, habitually uninformed, and the consummate sheep waiting to be sheared by dishonest and unethical professional politicians.

All the while, we live in a nation whereby voting itself has become a religiously spiritual holiday event where one gains a certain naively reassuring rite of passage as a patriotically credentialed adult, barrenly similar to finally being of legal drinking age.

All these Get Out the Vote campaigns are utter nonsense and end up being simple-minded political aphorisms which accomplish absolutely nothing of real substance.

Usually what these folks like MTV, famous celebrities, professional athletes, and political influencers mean with this social messaging is to vote according to some predetermined ideological belief structure such as vote Team Democrat or vote Team Republican, and not just to vote in general.

The assumption is that you are part of their team, see the world accordingly, and will vote along similar partisan party lines. Thus, Get Out the Vote really means to vote Liberal or Conservative, in other words, for our particular ideological side and the chosen and virtuous political party team. These voting advocates are effectively party cheerleaders for the cults of the Two-Party System.

But if we examine the status quo of the American voting system further, what kinds of candidates are routinely running for office, and the individuals being elected by these two political parties in this country. It is no accident that we essentially keep electing the same types of incompetent people and ineffective leaders over and over again.

So much is this obviously flawed methodological trend of electing terrible politicians that Americans are often compelled to vote in additional representatives from the same political families, spouses of elected leaders, and even their future offspring. In fact, there couldn't be more group think and narrow-minded decision making on behalf of the American voting public. It is almost as if the American voters are trying on purpose to elect the worst possible candidates for government office.

We have had Bush for eight years, Clinton for eight years, Obama for eight years, Reagan for eight years, we have had Democrats in office, Republicans in office, Conservatives, Liberals, Moderates, and it hasn't made any meaningful and substantive difference in the incompetent management of America.

The leaders from both political parties have failed miserably in balancing a budget, spending wisely, providing affordable housing, supporting healthcare needs, maintaining good roads, building important infrastructure projects such as high-speed rail and a modern electric grid, and thoughtfully planning for the future needs of this nation through cost effective and fundamentally sound policy measures.

What we really get regardless of who Americans vote for is politicians that become wealthier, giant corporations abusing the political system, more Americans becoming poorer, and larger legislative pork projects which America absolutely cannot afford.

We still have mass shootings, incredible societal violence, dangerous and filthy cities, tents under bridges, a large population of drug addicted citizens with many having mental health issues, panhandlers on every street corner, deteriorating roads and decaying infrastructure, increasingly pervasive taxation policies, continuously bigger government, thoroughly corrupt lobbying practices, and essentially outright bribery occurring on a regular basis in Washington.

This remains a never-ending list which includes continual partisan infighting in Congress, forever wars with young people dying needlessly to satisfy the wishes of the Military Industrial Complex, more government debt obligations, and a Federal Reserve that is propping up the entire financial Ponzi scheme that we mistakenly call capitalism in a desperate attempt to cling to an outdated identity which has long sense served its intended purpose and usefulness.

In principle, we are actively and knowingly denying the current broken state of the American economic and political system.

To be perfectly blunt, America has become a highly dysfunctional government subsidized by a thoroughly broken political system which represents an out-of-control corrupt bureaucracy that is categorically incompetent, creates additional systemic problems every year, and has been destroying this nation for the last 70 years at an ever-increasing rate of methodically efficient and self-defeating attacks on the very notion of democracy itself as a beacon in the night.

The overall quality of life for Americans has been on the decline for seven straight decades. In reality, America is being left behind on the world competitive stage by the likes of Australia, China, Germany, and South Korea. The United States of America is losing market share in many areas with regard to competitive dominance, and this is happening at an alarming rate in increasingly globalized markets.

All the while, Americans are too busy fighting amongst themselves, to even realize that they are being passed by on the world stage. In 30 years, the United States of America will be on the outside looking in at many global markets such as automobiles, electronics, agriculture, engineering, architecture, manufacturing, shipping, technology and even the entertainment industry.

This demise in American competitiveness around the world is even more striking considering the fact that America had such a significant head start over many of its competitors. This economic and political advantage was largely due to incredibly misguided socialistic practices and the deleterious effects of World War II on many of America's direct competitors in various markets.

In point of fact, at the current rate of decline in many of these industries and markets which America once dominated, there will be countless American businesses and important iconic companies that will be forced to cease operations in the foreseeable future.

The American economic and political climate appears rather bleak considering that our competitors are operating with a smarter business model which is better adapted to the current business environment and economic realities of the new world order.

Just look at the business models of China and South Korea, and how their government supports companies and industries which start competing on the global stage and ultimately conquer a given market.

Meanwhile, American businesses cannot even get private loans from banks these days.

The American government really has been asleep at the wheel in fostering genuine organic business growth in this country, and this remains especially true over the last 30 years of funny money economic policies.

So it stands high time that Americans arouse from their political slumber, as the global world is passing America by at an alarming rate. This all starts with the American citizens being informed voters.

In actuality, getting out the vote campaigns are utterly useless if most American voters have no real understanding of the issues which they are voting on in elections. We have so many uninformed voters making doltishly stupid voting decisions that elections have basically devolved into giant popularity contests for the uninitiated *Sheep*.

The entire system needs to be overhauled, and the news media with their irresponsible behaviors and often biased political agendas sure isn't helping the American voters be informed and objective agents on the actual fundamental issues facing this country.

As it stands now, the news media have become giant propaganda machines and bastions of misinformation. The news media is basically serving the purposeful function of a misinformation arm in a cult, and the cults are the two dominant political parties in this so-called representative democracy.

The modern American political system has participants acting like cult members. This is how bad things have gotten in our society today, with a voting public consisting of largely uninformed, unthinking *Sheep* that continually talk past one another, and miss the entire point of patriotic political participation.

We need to actually talk about the issues and get away from the Team Republican versus Team Democrat perspective and this "Us" versus "Them" political mentality in how we approach our patriotic participation and overall political thinking in

America.

The fundamental issues need to be laid out by objective analysts, and not partisan constituencies, corrupt and biased news media, thoroughly unscrupulous lobbyists, and dishonest career politicians who inevitably mislead the American voters by purposefully framing issues in untruthful terms through patently false and misleading information in order to push hidden and self-interested agendas.

These behind-the-scenes agendas often benefit prominent donors, large corporations, specific industries, the two dominant political parties, and other politically affiliated groups in Washington. This corrupted process leads to significant conflicts of interest vis-à-vis these important political issues.

It is quite apparent that many political issues are clouded and distorted by partisan propaganda campaigns, and that the American voters are routinely misinformed on the fundamental issues at the core of our political discussion, and this is primarily due to the powerfully corrupt and malevolent influences of our opaque, agenda driven political process.

Therefore, if voters cannot understand the full extent of the issues at hand in an objective and unbiased manner, then they are effectively unqualified to vote, and shouldn't be voting in political elections.

We make a real mistake in this country of celebrating the fact that we have uninformed, unqualified stupid people voting in our elections every political season, like this is a good thing.

It is a mistake to think that voting just for the sake of voting is something to uphold as a social good in this country. But we do this very thing right now. Indeed, the politicians love the fact that the average American voter is uninformed on the issues, as it makes their job a whole lot easier in manipulating the political system to their corrupt ends.

Hence, one of the first things that needs to be done to begin making positive political changes in this professed representative democracy is to start doing a better job of educating voters so that they are informed, intelligent participants in the political process who have the necessary tools to make good choices on the complex and difficult issues facing this inherently divided nation.

Once we achieve this ideal state of having informed and intelligent voters, then we can actually begin focusing on the fundamental issues, instead of Team Democrat versus Team Republican in these Super Bowl political events which are essentially sporting spectacles rather than political elections. In short, it's the issues stupid, focus on the issues!

However, in America's current political slumber, a bunch of mindlessly unthinking *Sheep* are being mercilessly manipulated by the current broken political system, and this needs to change. In effect, we have the incredibly incompetent and insanely stupid people running the government asylum right now in America.

If this unenlightened state of affairs continues you can kiss this country goodbye, as there truly stands no hope for humanity in the end. It remains an inescapable reality that without dramatic change, there is no promise for our political system, and absolutely no hope for America as a thriving democracy.

America is already a second-rate country on the absolute decline, and the counterfeit Democracy of the Two-Party System is the prime reason for this overwhelming government failure.

In point of fact, having too many stupid, uninformed, and

often hysterically emotional voters participating in our elections these days is certainly a recipe for political disaster. It stands as a political truism, and inevitably results in our broken political system that is failing most Americans right now.

In principle, voting ends up being manifestly nullified in the final analysis by brainless and woefully uninformed *Sheep* voters, powerful lobbyist groups, entrenched government bureaucrats, and corrupt backroom deals brokered by unethical career politicians who are all part and parcel of the familiarly broken, giant political cesspool of a system that we hubristically refer to as a representative democracy in this increasingly divisive and dying nation.

This serves as the basis for the logical reasoning behind the idea that voting doesn't really matter in America.

In sober fact, Washington, the Two-Party System, and Democracy as a political ideal doesn't work under the current social, economic, and political inputs.

It will take a political revolution in this country the likes of the Protestant Reformation to cause a significant paradigm shift where voting actually matters and legitimately makes a difference in our overall political system once again.

# 9 THE SAME OLD THING

I will start off this chapter with a little analogy to illustrate the incompetent nature of the United States Government these days. If you take a great architect or architecture firm, they have creative ideas in mind for projects, write out notes and put specifications on paper, produce detailed architectural drawings, and design the projects utilizing specialized computer software programs.

When large architecture firms have finished with the design phase, they supervise the hiring of engineering and procurement contractors, and ultimately work with the construction teams and materials contractors to ensure that the end product comes out according to the architectural designs as intended.

And when all is done, you end up with these great architectural masterpieces that are not only functional homes, inspiring workspaces, and iconic public buildings, but also incredible works of art in their own right.

In simple terms, there is something of value created, and something to show as the end product for all the hard work, intellectual creativity, and financial resources that were invested into the making of these architectural projects.

Now let us contrast this with Washington's spending, and all the time and effort they put into government projects which in the end have very little of substantive value to show for these expensive and expansive activities.

It is quite revealing how frequently there is no end product which everyone can appreciate and understand that results from Washington's efforts, unlike that of great architectural works.

For example, the United States Government spent around two trillion dollars in Iraq since the invasion in 2003.[73] I am not sure that you can call it a war, who were we exactly fighting in Iraq?

It sure wasn't the Iraqi military, as the United States military always seems to find these *boogeyman enemies* whenever they invade a country, which essentially represent no threat to the citizenry back home in America. Therefore, the fair question remains, what did America truly accomplish with this invasion of Iraq?

This was almost like the classic Franklin D. Roosevelt's Works Progress Administration program of paying workers to dig holes and then filling them back up again.[74] Furthermore, other figures point to the United States Government spending $6.4 trillion for military activities in Afghanistan, Iraq, Syria, and Pakistan.[75]

---

[73] https://www.militarytimes.com/opinion/commentary/2020/02/06/the-iraq-war-has-cost-the-us-nearly-2-trillion/; https://en.wikipedia.org/wiki/Financial_cost_of_the_Iraq_War

[74] https://en.wikipedia.org/wiki/Works_Progress_Administration; https://www.encyclopedia.com/education/news-and-education-magazines/works-progress-administration-1935-1943

[75] https://www.cnbc.com/2019/11/20/us-spent-6point4-trillion-on-middle-

Let me reiterate that I am not sure who we are actually fighting in any of these countries, so I really cannot call these particular military activities *Wars*. I mean seriously, it isn't like Afghanistan has a fleet of aircraft carriers and an actual military.

But there are numerous reports of our oversized military wasting tons of money in these countries, and all of this bureaucratic waste, exorbitant military spending, outright defense fraud, and fiscal mismanagement is paid for by the gullibly uninformed American taxpayers.[76]

In other words, what does America have to show for all this taxpayer spending? Has anything materially changed in any of these countries? What did we create in these countries? What beautiful architectural masterpieces can we go visit in any of these countries?

We have a large number of injured soldiers returning home to try and put their lives back together after these military activities in foreign lands. We have spent an enormously large amount of taxpayer money buying military equipment and building temporary military bases in these countries which will inevitably be abandoned down the line.

We made a fortune for military contractors and the defense industry during this time. But these are private and public companies, what does America have to show for all this wasted political effort, decades of lost time, and immense capital resources that are continually invested into these manufactured

---

east-wars-since-2001-study.html
[76] https://www.stripes.com/news/fraud-waste-and-abuse-cost-us-19-billion-in-one-decade-in-afghanistan-1.649357;
https://www.pbs.org/newshour/show/report-finds-fraud-waste-by-war-contractors-costs-billions;
https://www.nbcnews.com/news/military/watchdog-says-u-s-wasted-more-15-billion-past-11-n894701

military activities and woefully ineffective industrial defense projects.

And let's be forthright, these aren't actual wars, these are spuriously constructed military projects. Although more to the point, the United States Military is in actuality a giant business corporation like Apple and Microsoft, and heavily involved in massive business development activities and highly creative marketing campaigns cloaked under the ghostly guise of national security concerns.

In this country, we have made rational thinking a shameful act, as one can never question military activities and defense spending. If you don't support "Forever Wars" in America, then you are being an unpatriotic citizen.

The heavily lobbied career politicians in Washington on both sides of the partisan isle never question the reasoning behind defense spending, these nonsensical military campaigns, and the perpetual wars that have no real objectives and continue on long past their original political purpose.

There are the standard responses that you are just militarily naïve, and you don't understand the complex history of wars and overall military theory. Along these lines, you are simply a civilian, and private citizens could not possibly understand the importance and necessity of these military operations.

In other words, we are the military experts, we are well versed in military history, and we are the heavily credentialed military professionals. Therefore, how dare you question our ideas and judge our results!

Let's be perfectly clear here, we do this for a living, and you don't, so shut up and continue being the good little enablers of our incessant warmongering. The bottom line is that you stupid little *Sheep* should never question our authority on military matters, and your only role is to keep giving us endless rivers of taxpayer money, with absolutely no accountability whatsoever, got that?

This is basically the argument used to justify the military status quo of continually finding "Forever Wars" to commit American taxpayers to funding in a never-ending cycle of nothingness. I call it nothingness because when all is said and done, America has nothing to show for all of these poorly managed military activities and profoundly misused taxpayer dollars.

The analogy that I started this chapter out with applies to many areas of our government such as the education system where American students are critically falling behind the rest of the world.[77] We collect all this taxpayer money, and pile enormous sums of financial resources into the American education system, and yet we continue to get rather poor results on the whole.

I swear kids would get a better education just by spending a couple of hours a day on the free online website Khan Academy.[78] The American education system has become a bastion of politics itself, so in a sense, the very problem with our overly political government model is being replicated in the schools and the overall education system in this country.

No one thinks that we are doing a good job of educating students and school children in this seemingly developed nation. Again, the education system in America serves as a prime example of taking in a whole lot of resources on the

---

[77] https://www.thebalance.com/the-u-s-is-losing-its-competitive-advantage-3306225; https://www.weforum.org/agenda/2017/02/us-students-are-lagging-behind-academically-heres-why

[78] https://www.khanacademy.org/

input side of the equation and having nothing really beautiful to look at on the output side of the equation.

This is symptomatic of an incompetently run country, as we never have something good to show for our considerable time and resources devoted to government outcomes.

The United States of America epitomizes a thoroughly mismanaged and highly corrupt, pseudo capitalistic representative democracy which is moving at breakneck speed towards a head on collision with the treacherously beguiling oasis of a demonically authoritarian, socialistically dystopian nightmare also known as the promised land for many career politicians.

In truth, we are fundamentally a failing nation governed by incompetent people and corrupt leaders. If there is one thing that America does really good, it is fully embracing and promoting incompetency as a primary value, we have that cultural skillset and overriding guiding principle mastered to the interminable core of this dying nation.

Another domain where America doesn't produce good government outcomes is in the area of healthcare. The United States ranks very poorly on most World Healthcare Rankings based upon many metrics like spending allocation costs, quality of care, affordability, and overall coverage for Americans.[79]

For example, the United States of America spends more on healthcare than any other country in the world, and yet gets far worse outcomes by a substantial margin.[80] Strictly speaking, to

---

[79] https://worldpopulationreview.com/country-rankings/best-healthcare-in-the-world; https://www.citizen.org/article/dead-last-u-s-health-care-system-continues-to-rank-behind-other-industrialized-countries/; https://www.numbeo.com/health-care/rankings_by_country.jsp
[80] https://www.commonwealthfund.org/publications/issue-

say that the American healthcare system is broken would be a considerable understatement, even under the most charitable light.

The issue has become highly politicized by both parties to manipulate voters through means of misdirection which effectively takes their eyes off the real problems with our healthcare system and the venal government leaders who are largely responsible for this incompetent state of affairs in this critically important industry over these irretrievably lost decades of failed public policy.

Again, healthcare is an area where we spend a great deal of time and resources in this nation and have absolutely nothing of comparable value or wonderful outcomes to show for our government efforts in this purported free market economy.

I can tell you who is benefiting from this thoroughly corrupt system, the big business interests in the healthcare industry, i.e., insurance companies, pharmaceutical cartels, medical device firms, healthcare institutions, and public health bureaucrats.

There are a whole group of industry insiders getting filthy rich off this broken and flawed healthcare system in our counterfeit representative democracy. In stark contrast, the American people as a whole are the ones truly suffering from this decidedly broken and clearly failing system which has maliciously mutated with the tyrannical support of rotten public policy out of Washington.

Once more, America has mastered the art of incompetency to perfection! We are extremely good at accomplishing incompetent results and producing terrible outcomes in literally

---

briefs/2020/jan/us-health-care-global-perspective-2019; https://www.apha.org/topics-and-issues/health-rankings

every sector or industry which our oversized government touches through its vast bureaucratic arms and authoritarian reach.

I could literally go down almost every sector in our government driven economy from agriculture and energy policymaking, infrastructure projects, parks and recreation spending, managing homeland security, all the way to costly expenditures for space exploration at NASA, and we will get the same story told over and over again in this precariously positioned debt-ridden nation.

We never have very much to show in the end from all of our efforts and resources, there is rarely a nice beautiful lasting accomplishment that we can all see and share as Americans at the end of this government rainbow.

America is mastering one thing in this process, the skill of being perpetually incompetent. Let's face this fact, right now America is an incompetent nation, and it starts with Washington and our political leaders, the ruling class in this country, who are the epitome of incompetent people.

We continue to elect the same old incompetent people to lead this nation in Washington year after year. Thus, the first step to eliminating this incompetency phase in American history, is to start electing more competent leaders in government.

So let's start off with describing the typical candidates who run for political office in this nominal representative democracy. If we examine the presidents that we have elected to lead this nation, they all basically fit the same prototypical person.

We will start with John F. Kennedy in 1961, as there has been a definitive decline in many areas of this country that began around the decade of the 1960s. John F. Kennedy graduated from Harvard University, came from a politically connected family, and would absolutely fit in the category of looking for political fame, pursuing power, and seeking positional status as a human being from a basic motivation standpoint.[81]

Shoot, the entire Kennedy family embodied this lust for political power, as they practically sent every member of their family to serve in some form of government office from Congress to the American Presidency.

Next came Lyndon B. Johnson from 1963-1969, Lyndon B. Johnson was a career politician who worked his way up the political ladder, serving in the House of Representatives from 1937-1949, transitioned to being a US Senator representing the state of Texas from 1949-1961, moved up another level to Vice President from 1961-1963, and became President of the United States after the assassination of John F. Kennedy.[82]

Again, Lyndon B. Johnson's entire life was defined through participating in a career revolving around politics, and he obviously loved the fame, status, and power that politics provided, not to mention the secretive underworld of backroom deals.[83]

We close out the 1960s with Richard Nixon as President from 1969-1974, and not surprisingly Richard Nixon began his professional career as a lawyer before entering the unscrupulous world of politics.

Richard Nixon was another career politician in the final

---


[81] https://en.wikipedia.org/wiki/John_F._Kennedy

[82] https://en.wikipedia.org/wiki/Lyndon_B._Johnson

[83] https://www.npr.org/2012/11/11/164894065/leading-in-crisis-lessons-from-lyndon-johnson; https://www.purdue.edu/convocations/how-to-get-power/

analysis, first serving as a member of the House of Representatives for California from 1947-1950, gravitating to the United States Senate from 1950-1953, becoming Vice President from 1953-1961 under Dwight D. Eisenhower, and finally fulfilling his career ambitions in 1969 with the American Presidency.[84]

Once more, as we can behold, these presidents are all essentially the same types of individuals, they often served in the military, had legal backgrounds, were from prominent and wealthy families, demonstrated a strong lust for power, and were fundamentally career politicians.

After Richard Nixon was forced out of office due to the Watergate scandal, Gerald Ford moved into the Presidency from 1974-1977. He went to Yale Law School, served in the military, and became a member of the House of Representatives from 1949-1973, was House Minority Leader from 1965-1973, served as Vice President under Richard Nixon from 1973-1974, and ultimately became President of the United States in 1974.[85]

These presidents are essentially cookie cutter candidates from the same political mold, career politicians who deftly moved up the political ladder, and it is no real surprise that these presidents left a legacy of bad government policies in their wake as inept leaders in this thoroughly declining nation.

As a matter of fact, I wouldn't call any of these people particularly competent at their jobs as presidents in this gravely failing democracy. Not a single president stemmed the obvious deterioration in the overall American standard of living which has been on the precipitous decline from its peak established

---

[84] https://en.wikipedia.org/wiki/Richard_Nixon
[85] https://en.wikipedia.org/wiki/Gerald_Ford

during the 1950s.

We move next to Jimmy Carter who was President from 1977-1981. He attended the U.S. Naval Academy, was from a wealthy family, and his father served in the Georgia House of Representatives.

Jimmy Carter was a Georgia State Senator from 1963-1967, became Governor of Georgia from 1971-1975, and ultimately reached the American Presidency in 1977.[86] In principle, we haven't deviated from the prototypical presidential candidate yet in this little history exercise.

In the decade of the 1980s, Ronald Reagan was President for most of those years, as he held the American Presidency from 1981-1989. Ronald Reagan started his professional career as an actor, he also served in the military, was president of the Screen Actors Guild, and became heavily involved in politics during the 1950s and 1960s.

Ronald Reagan was elected and served as Governor of California from 1967-1975, inevitably setting his political sights at the national level, and ultimately succeeded in becoming President of the United States in 1981.[87]

It may appear that Ronald Reagan is something different, even a political outsider, but make no mistake, Ronald Reagan was a force in California politics for a long time, and in the end was absolutely a career politician.

And like the presidents before him during this politically purblind era of America's decline, Ronald Reagan left a rather substantial legacy of failed policy initiatives during his overly romanticized tenure in office.

---

[86] https://en.wikipedia.org/wiki/Jimmy_Carter; https://en.wikipedia.org/wiki/James_Earl_Carter_Sr.
[87] https://en.wikipedia.org/wiki/Ronald_Reagan

We next move to George H. W. Bush who served as President from 1989-1993. He also served in the military, was from an important and wealthy family, and went to Yale University. George H. W. Bush became wealthy in business through the oil industry, was elected to the House of Representatives in the late 1960s, and subsequently lost a bid for the United States Senate in 1970.[88]

George H. W. Bush was appointed Ambassador to the United Nations by Richard Nixon in the early 1970s, became chairman of the Republican National Committee, was selected as the U.S. envoy to the People's Republic of China, and eventually served as the director of the Central Intelligence Agency in 1976.

Finally, George H. W. Bush was selected and worked as Vice President under Ronald Reagan from 1981-1989, and ultimately reached his political goal of the American Presidency in 1989.[89]

We literally can check the following boxes with these political candidates: Influential & Wealthy Families, Ivy League Education, Military Service, and of course, the all-important Career Politicians. Yes, we definitely have *A Ruling Class* in this country.

We find ourselves in the midst of a string of two term presidents with Bill Clinton serving from 1993-2001. Bill Clinton went to Yale Law School, was Governor of Arkansas from 1979-1981, and then again from 1983-1992, and eventually became President of the United States in 1993.[90]

Bill Clinton had political aspirations and ambitions for the highest office in America from a relatively early age.[91] Once

---


[88] https://millercenter.org/president/bush/life-before-the-presidency
[89] https://en.wikipedia.org/wiki/George_H._W._Bush
[90] https://en.wikipedia.org/wiki/Bill_Clinton
[91] https://millercenter.org/president/clinton/life-before-the-presidency

more, we find that Bill Clinton checks many of the same boxes as prior presidents who cannot seem to resist the intoxicating allure of the American Presidency.

Bill Clinton was definitely seduced by the fame, status, and power awarded to its political victors, and like most career politicians in Washington he became a very wealthy person through political service to the country.

The new millennium is the same as the old millennium in this counterfeit representative democracy, and we become fully vested in the new millennium with the Presidency of George W. Bush.

George W. Bush was President from 2001-2009, went to Yale University, attained an MBA from Harvard Business School, and not unexpectedly served in the military. George W. Bush became wealthy through some sweetheart business deals afforded to him primarily because he was from an important and influential political family.[92]

George W. Bush suffered a loss in his first attempt at politics when he ran for the House of Representatives on behalf of Texas during 1978, gained further political experience working on his father's presidential campaigns in 1988 and 1992, and was eventually elected Governor of Texas from 1995-2000. And finally, George W. Bush became President of the United States in 2001.[93]

The younger Bush was just going into the family business, probably thinking that he inherited a natural birthright to the American Presidency like the rest of the Bush offspring.

---

[92] https://millercenter.org/president/gwbush/life-before-the-presidency; https://www.tampabay.com/archive/2000/10/29/influence-and-bailouts-a-business-tradition-in-bush-family/

[93] https://en.wikipedia.org/wiki/George_W._Bush

George W. Bush was probably right, after all, he was basically a member of the ruling class in this country. How do you think he got into the Ivy League in the first place, it was obviously the result of being a legacy candidate.[94]

George W. Bush sure did his part to push the agenda of the Military Industrial Complex and Forever Wars at an extraordinarily high cost to the American taxpayers and soldiers deployed in foreign countries. George W. Bush practically invented the terminology 'shortsighted leadership' during his incompetent tenure as President of the United States.

We move from George W. Bush to that of Barack Obama, who was President from 2009-2017. Barack Obama was another two-term president and attended Columbia University and Harvard Law School. Barack Obama taught law for 12 years at the University of Chicago Law School, had community organizing experience, and eventually became an Illinois State Senator from 1997-2004.

Barack Obama served as a U.S. Senator from the state of Illinois during the time period of 2005-2008, and ultimately became President of the United States in 2009.[95]

Barack Obama majored in political science while at Columbia University, and if you don't think he had political ambitions about being President of the United States while at Harvard Law School, then I have some prime swampland in Louisiana to sell you.[96]

Once again, although Barack Obama was the first African American elected to the Presidency, he still checks many of the boxes of the ruling class that is continually elected to the highest

---

[94] https://www.nytimes.com/2004/09/13/opinion/the-legacy-of-legacies.html
[95] https://en.wikipedia.org/wiki/Barack_Obama
[96] https://millercenter.org/president/obama/life-before-the-presidency

political office in this failing democracy.

And like George W. Bush before him, he blew out the fiscal budget in an already heavily indebted nation with some ridiculously bad government policies, including bailouts of the financial markets, and continual support for military campaigns that made no sense from an objectives standpoint.

We move next to Donald Trump who was President from 2017-2021. Donald Trump tries to portray himself as a political outsider, but this is purely a marketing ploy on his behalf, as Donald Trump is as much of an insider as any of the other candidates for president that we have covered in this chapter.

Donald Trump went to the Wharton School of Business at the University of Pennsylvania. He came from a wealthy family, was set up in the real estate business through his father and made/inherited a lot of money through various connected means. Donald Trump was involved in many high-profile business ventures from Atlantic City casinos to the United States Football League.[97]

Donald Trump was a savvy media insider who had access to many politicians in both parties. He switched political parties when it suited his interests and was vocal about many political issues for decades before actually running for elected office.

Donald Trump already had plenty of experience in the media, which was bolstered by his hit reality show on television *The Apprentice*. In practice, Donald Trump was a famous and well-known celebrity in society for decades, and he used this brand recognition and celebrity status to his advantage in successfully running for President of the United States.[98]

---

[97] https://en.wikipedia.org/wiki/Donald_Trump;
https://en.wikipedia.org/wiki/United_States_Football_League
[98] https://en.wikipedia.org/wiki/The_Apprentice_(American_TV_series)

And if you think Donald Trump didn't have ambitions on the American Presidency for the purpose of attaining more fame, power, status, and wealth, then you are a very naïve and gullible person.[99] It sure wasn't to make America a better country.

These are the exact wrong kind of individuals that should be serving in public office. It's really all about them, not the good of the nation.

In the final analysis, Donald Trump is no political outsider, despite how he markets himself to the American voters. Moreover, Donald Trump's policies also reflect those of previous political insiders, as one of the first things he did while in office was to give sizable tax cuts to large corporations.[100]

These large corporations are already failing to pay their fair share of taxes through the considerable corporate tax loopholes that lower their effective tax rate obligations to criminal levels when you get right down to it.[101] Furthermore, America couldn't afford these tax cuts to large corporations, as the budget deficit hit record highs during the Trump Presidency, and this was even before the effects of the Covid-19 Lockdowns.[102]

---

[99] https://www.npr.org/2017/01/20/510680463/donald-trumps-been-saying-the-same-thing-for-30-years

[100] https://www.nbcnews.com/politics/politics-news/trump-signs-tax-cut-bill-first-big-legislative-win-n832141; https://www.americanprogress.org/issues/economy/news/2019/09/26/475083/trumps-corporate-tax-cut-not-trickling/

[101] https://fortune.com/2019/12/19/low-effective-corporate-tax-rates/; https://www.americanprogress.org/issues/economy/news/2020/10/28/492473/6-ways-trump-administration-rigging-already-unfair-tax-code/

[102] https://www.cnbc.com/2019/09/12/budget-deficit-smashes-1-trillion-mark-the-highest-in-seven-years.html; https://www.bloombergquint.com/politics/trump-s-soaring-budget-deficit-

And people wonder why I argue that we are going broke as a nation, it is because the American voters continue to act like a flock of sheep and keep electing politicians from the ruling class, and the failed policy measures of the ruling class speak for themselves.

We finally move to the last president in this discussion with Joe Biden who will become the 46th President of the United States in January of 2021. Joe Biden has said that he will only seek one term in office. However, Joe Biden has flipflopped on this one term in office issue like only a career politician in Washington could do so brazenly.

Frankly, after watching Joe Biden in office for the first year, I am not sure Biden remembers what he said two weeks ago, let alone on the campaign trail.[103]

In summary, Joe Biden is another career politician, he went to Law School at Syracuse University, was politically active in his local community, and was elected to the United States Senate representing Delaware and served in Congress from 1973-2009.

Joe Biden ran for president in 2008, became Vice President under Barack Obama from 2009-2017, and ultimately reached his political ambitions of becoming President of the United States in November, and was sworn into office on January 20,

---

risks-intensifying-market-frenzy;
https://www.marketwatch.com/story/trump-added-about-3-9-trillion-to-deficits-so-far-budget-group-says-11599669921
[103] https://www.politico.com/news/2019/12/11/biden-single-term-082129; https://www.usnews.com/news/elections/articles/2019-12-11/joe-biden-suggests-he-would-only-serve-one-term-if-elected-president; https://www.npr.org/2021/03/25/981260663/biden-says-he-expects-to-run-for-a-second-term

2021.[104]

Joe Biden is the quintessential career politician, and unfortunately his candidacy embodies everything that is wrong with our current political system. He has served for five decades in Washington, and during this period the country as a whole has been on a rather precipitous decline.

In more complex terms, Washington as an institution has been an absolute political disaster symbolic of a dysfunctional paradigm fictitiously masquerading as a responsible government during his entire time hopelessly serving in public office.

Joe Biden checks off many of the same boxes as the previous presidents of the last 70 years in this professed representative democracy: lawyer, career politician, became wealthy through politics in Washington, and chosen member of the ruling class.[105]

Maybe the American voters should think differently about the types of individuals they perceive as good candidates for elected office. I didn't see too many nerdy bookkeepers over the course of our discussion.

It is evident that Joe Biden is more concerned about his political ambitions and future legacy as the 46th President of the United States, as opposed to whether he is even fit to be in office at his advanced age and overall poor health.

The fact that the American people elected a person who is having major cognitive difficulties just remembering basic facts

---

[104] https://en.wikipedia.org/wiki/Joe_Biden

[105] https://www.townandcountrymag.com/society/politics/a31265187/joe-biden-net-worth/; https://www.opensecrets.org/2020-presidential-race/joe-biden/candidate?id=N00001669; https://www.cnbc.com/2019/07/12/how-joe-biden-became-a-millionaire.html

that he is prepped on each day is rather shocking on its own, but it is obvious that Joe Biden is in no shape to hold one of the most demanding jobs on the planet, let alone actually excel in the position.[106]

Candidly, it will be a miracle if Joe Biden can actually finish out his four-year term in office at the rate which his physical and mental health is deteriorating right before our eyes. In any event, it is clear just based upon his cabinet picks so far that the lobbying industry will feel right at home in a Biden Presidency.

And why shouldn't this be the case, as Joe Biden is the consummate political insider in Washington, and he has been a part of the lobbying cesspool and political establishment in our massively failing government bureaucracy his entire five-decade long career as a so-called public servant.

The only person that Joe Biden has ever served in government is himself, period. It sure hasn't been the American people.

When in doubt, just follow the money, and Joe Biden is the ultimate, corrupt career politician in Washington.[107] Remember, by definition if you are a career politician, then you are de facto a corrupt politician in my book.

The assumption and logic that I am relying upon with this statement, is that having a long career in Washington these days means that you have learned how to play the political game, and

---

[106] https://www.bu.edu/articles/2020/oldest-president-elected-joe-biden/
[107] https://www.foxnews.com/politics/plausible-deniability-tony-bobulinski-biden-family; https://www.foxnews.com/politics/graham-hunter-biden-business-industrial-scale-corruption; https://www.politico.com/magazine/story/2019/08/02/joe-biden-investigation-hunter-brother-hedge-fund-money-2020-campaign-227407; https://nypost.com/2020/11/01/how-joe-biden-clearly-benefited-from-biden-family-business/

the political game in Washington is all about corruption, whether we are talking implicitly or explicitly.

How fitting to end this discussion of American Presidents over the last 70 years, with the American *Sheep* voters continuing to elect the exact wrong kind of people to serve in Washington, as these politicians are all essentially created from the same cookie-cutter mold.

The ruling class is definitely represented quite well with a Joe Biden Presidency. Yes indeed, more of *The Same Old Thing* in Washington Politics. This is why our country is in such dire straits right now.

In summation, we have just covered the presidents for the last 70 years in our self-styled democratic nation, and if we analyzed the United States Congress, we would find similar patterns regarding *The Same Old Thing*, and the same types of stereotypical politicians and self-interested personalities being elected to office decade after futile decade in American politics.

This needs to stop, as we elect the worst sort of individuals for elective office. In truth, the American people have bad taste when it comes to political candidates. We pass over the good ones in favor of the bad ones on a regular basis, which makes for a really poor democracy.

It seems that if we cast a Venn diagram over our political ruling class that not only will we discover that these people have many things in common, that in effect, they are always the exact wrong kind of individuals who should be serving in government.

But we would also find another common characteristic, these people are largely incompetent in life. Thus, if it weren't for politics, what skillset or private sector job which required real competency would these political characters actually excel at working outside of government?

This idea of basic competency is a big problem in our culture at large, as we have undoubtedly become an incompetent country in so many areas of our society. We have become fat, happy, complacent, and thoroughly soft as a nation, and this mentality permeates almost every aspect of the American society.

It is just extremely hard to find anyone who executes their craft, duty, or profession in a competent manner these days. By and large, finding someone who has a definitive track record of consistently performing their job or particular role in society at a competent level nowadays usually requires a certain type of distinctive character.

These individuals care about doing and completing their work in a competent manner because their personal makeup in essence demands it, and this is all apart from monetary or extrinsic factors of motivation. Discovering people with a high level of intrinsic drive is the real holy grail in our modern world.

To be sure, these are rare birds in our society today, as most encounters that one has with the services sector of the economy, and the United States is largely a service-based economy, are routinely filled with massive inefficiencies and widespread incompetence. It is quite apparent that America has become hopelessly enamored with the dark clouds of incompetence.

What's more, this isn't a class specific problem as doctors, lawyers, finance professionals, business managers, and corporate executives are largely incompetent at their jobs.

We literally have a plague of incompetency wreaking havoc in America, so much so, that when someone just does their job in a competent manner, it stands out like a miracle of creation.

We are amazed that things actually went according to plan.

In our society, most people just do things the way they want, usually this means getting the job done with the least possible thought, effort, and time spent on the task at hand, they really don't care or think about whether this is performing the job in a competent manner. This is one of the reasons why Americans are so uninformed on political issues.

And when the results end up being extremely poor as expected, these incompetent people will just lie, cheat, and work twice as hard justifying their original efforts and terrible performance, as opposed to simply undoing the bad policy or fixing the original mistake.

This is all hilariously irrational behavior, because in many cases it is much easier to just admit that they made a mistake and fix the problem, versus all the time and energy they spend in psychological denial, effectively going out of their way to defend the incompetence.

This is highly ironic behavior, because this head in the sand approach, only adds to the incompetence of the original problem. It is simply reinforcing or doubling down on their incompetency.

Actually, these individuals couldn't be any more self-sabotaging if they tried purposely to be incompetent at their jobs, endeavors, or political policies. This concept perfectly personifies the Joe Biden presidency after reviewing his first year in office.

This is basically the American society in a nutshell these days, and the ruling class in Washington embodies this incompetence fault more than any other sector in our economy. So why is this the case?

This is due to the fact that these career politicians and

professional bureaucrats are not particularly competent at doing anything productive in general, and this is why they chose to participate and stay in politics and government until they are literally dragged out of Washington kicking and screaming.

Indeed, what is the old saying that politics is showbiz for ugly people, I am beginning to think that politics and government are really the place for stupid, untalented fraudsters who cannot do anything else in this world.[108]

This country undoubtedly gives far too much of a voice and subsequent power to genuinely stupid people who aren't qualified to manage any small business concern, let alone in deciding public policy for the United States of America.

In reality, Washington is full of untalented, highly incompetent political and bureaucratic hacks who have been ruining this country through their sheer incompetent actions in government for decades. These individuals are not in government to serve Americans, they are in positions of power strictly to serve themselves.

The good *Doctor of Science*, the saintly Dr. Anthony Fauci comes to mind here, the purest example of a useless bureaucratic hack, one who makes everything he touches worse off in the process.[109] His long career in Washington, only helps bolster the case for a greatly slimmed down government going

---

[108]

https://www.barrypopik.com/index.php/new_york_city/entry/politics_is_show_business_for_ugly_people; http://voices.washingtonpost.com/reliable-source/2010/12/who_says_washington_is_hollywo.html

[109] https://www.newsweek.com/fauci-untruthful-congress-wuhan-lab-research-documents-show-gain-function-1627351; https://www.washingtonexaminer.com/news/here-are-faucis-biggest-flip-flops-and-backtracks-amid-the-coronavirus-pandemic; https://www.amazon.com/Do-Pray-Tell-Anthony-Prayer/dp/B086JBHS9H

forward in America.

These are the exact wrong kinds of people that we need in government. It is another bitter irony of humanity and societies in general, that the people who want to work in politics, are the exact wrong kind of people to have this responsibility, and the people who don't want to work in politics, are the exact people needed for these government roles and responsibilities.

So it is obvious that we do not have a government which represents a Meritocracy based upon the following meaning: "This is a political system in which economic goods and political power are vested in individual people on the basis of talent, effort, and achievement, rather than wealth or social class."[110]

Let's examine another definition for Meritocracy in the following: "a system, organization, or society in which people are chosen and moved into positions of success, power, and influence on the basis of their demonstrated abilities and merit."[111]

This idea of Meritocracy is contrasted with the Ruling Class which is defined as the following: "The class of people from which a country's rulers or government are typically drawn; a society's powerful or elite considered collectively."[112]

Some other definitions for the Ruling Class are the following: "The ruling class is the social class of a given society that decides upon and sets that society's political agenda."[113] And this notion is also straightforwardly expressed as, "The

---

[110] https://en.wikipedia.org/wiki/Meritocracy
[111] https://www.merriam-webster.com/dictionary/meritocracy
[112] https://www.lexico.com/en/definition/ruling_class
[113] https://en.wikipedia.org/wiki/Ruling_class

most powerful people in a country."[114]

This description of the Ruling Class best characterizes our government representatives in Washington these days, we sure don't have a Meritocracy with regard to the leaders in our government.

Do you really think that Nancy Pelosi, Alexandria Ocasio-Cortez, Mitch McConnell, and Lindsey Graham are in Washington because they are competent people who pass responsible legislation for the good of the country?

This is the Peter Principle at work here, which can be defined as follows: "the principle that members of a hierarchy are promoted until they reach the level at which they are no longer competent."[115]

I use this Peter Principle concept as a basis for discussing incompetence in general, but I employ a different perspective on it.

We will call this the Incompetence Principle which I define as incompetent individuals like to hire and surround themselves with other likewise incompetent people so that they don't stand out as being highly incompetent. This way they are not threatened by having competent people continually exposing the harsh reality that they are incompetent individuals.

This is the reason why competent people often don't get hired for positions, because the hiring managers realize that these people will make them look bad and could eventually take their jobs.

Likewise, there is little doubt that individuals who run for political office in Washington are usually highly incompetent.

---

[114] https://dictionary.cambridge.org/us/dictionary/english/ruling-class
[115] https://languages.oup.com/google-dictionary-en/

In truth, this represents their best career option, a job with no actual accountability.

This all plays out with these incompetent politicians inevitably hiring an entire staff of equally incompetent people so as not to feel personally threatened by any notion and standard of competence while in office.

The net result is that we have an entire cesspool of political incompetents working in our government passing terrible legislation which has been steadily destroying this nation over the last 70 years.

This failing government bureaucracy propagates like a highly virulent virus, and we end up with an incompetent Ruling Class in Washington making incredibly stupid decisions for the increasingly unraveling democracy which uncontrollably feeds off itself with dire consequences. In truth, an incompetent government is the single greatest factor in America's sharp decline on the global stage.

Hence, the definition of incompetence is the following: "The inability to do something successfully; ineptitude."[116] And the definition for competence is as follows: "The quality or state of having sufficient knowledge, judgment, skill, or strength (as for a particular duty or in a particular respect)."[117]

Well, we know that Washington is incapable of passing a respectable and balanced budget, i.e., living within their financial means.

And it is going to require a different kind of political animal in our government to start producing competent actions and taking proactive steps towards turning this wayward ship

---

[116] https://languages.oup.com/google-dictionary-en/
[117] https://www.merriam-webster.com/dictionary/competence

around strictly from a budgetary and fiscal spending standpoint.

Let alone in addressing the much more difficult and complex problems that this fatally divided, and thoroughly demoralized nation faces right now.

The solution is to find people who have a solid history of performing their duties, particular craft and chosen profession in a highly competent manner. The reality stands that we need basic competency more than anything else in government right now.

For instance, do potential political candidates have a consistent track record of achieving competent work? This remains the fundamental question to ask of future politicians.

In fact, these people probably are not politicians or political candidates at all, but professionals in other fields who have demonstrated a long history of being competent individuals. More specifically, these accomplished citizens make decisions and take actions appropriate for effectively solving problems and completing important project goals in a competent, efficient, and timely manner.

Find these types of individuals in society and give these people four years in Washington to get things done as civil servants for their country.[118] Because trust me, this failing democracy desperately needs these valued civil servants, as there are no competent people in politics these days.

By recruiting citizens who don't aspire to work in Washington or a career in politics, we start getting the right kind of individuals that can work together to solve difficult problems.

These civil servants who are not motivated by political

---

[118] Bear in mind that I am using 'civil servants' here in a nontraditional way.

ambitions or partisan concerns have a much greater chance of actually getting important things done in government which are objectively good for the country.

We of course, contrast this commonsense approach with continuing to do *The Same Old Thing* in Washington, and somehow miraculously expecting different results.

America has been consistently getting poor government policy outcomes over the last 70 years with this clearly systemically flawed approach towards the selection of *professional politicians* to govern our political system. It is time for change.

I titled this book *Sheep*, and in some sense, this is being a little harsh on the American people and voters in our political system. This is because Americans have their own demanding lives to lead which takes up most of their time and energy, and frankly they don't have the requisite ability to make the corrupt and incompetent political representatives in Washington accountable for their bad behavior.

Furthermore, most Americans have no idea the depth of this country's problems and the role that politicians have played in creating many of these government manufactured crises. And the news media and journalism industry as a whole sure isn't helping matters with providing informative, non-biased coverage of Washington Politics, and educating voters on the various social, economic, and political issues facing this troubled nation.

The news media and journalism industry is more concerned about pushing partisan agendas on both sides of the political aisle, getting ratings and subscriptions at all costs, and being well thought of in their social circles.

The last thing on the minds of news media and journalists these days is actually providing objective facts and information on Politics so that their audiences are well-informed on important issues to make good decisions with their political choices come election season.

However, in another sense, I am not being hard enough on the American voters because frankly you are complete idiots for continuing to vote these corrupt and incompetent politicians in Washington for decades without learning from your mistakes.

The fact that the American voters get all excited every election season, that this year will be different, and will bring about meaningful change in Washington is rather pathetic.

I understand that some of these individuals are slick salespeople, and the giant political machinery of the Two-Party System is also working against the American voters with their partisan propaganda efforts, but still this is not rocket science folks.

For example, quit doing the same thing over and over again and expecting different or better results in Washington. It hasn't worked for the last 70 years, and it isn't going to work for the next 70 years if we don't start doing something different in our failing democracy.

Part of the problem remains that the wrong kinds of people aspire to work in Politics, so voters' choices are rather limited, no matter who they send to Washington, as in the end, they are still getting the same types of professional politicians in government decade after ineffective decade.

In other words, the candidates voters didn't send to Washington probably wouldn't be much better than the shady scoundrels they actually voted into elected office to supposedly serve this withering republic.

The other contributing factor to this voting failure on behalf of America, stands that the system itself is built with a lot of misaligned incentives such as lobbying, bureaucratic self-preservation tendencies, lack of term limits, and no real accountabilities or consequences for incompetent performance on behalf of unscrupulous career politicians.

We need to take the Politics out of government and

legislative policymaking, as essentially right now both sides of the political spectrum are largely just talking past one another. In this broadly divided nation, we have to start working together, find areas of agreement, vital common ground, and work as a unified team towards solving difficult problems.

The reality exists that Americans are so busy fighting against each other that they fail to realize who the real enemies are in this dying republic. The common citizens as a unified and nonpartisan majority need to rise up against the incompetent ruling class before it is entirely too late.

The real enemies in America are the corrupt career politicians, our massive government bureaucracy, big tech oligarchies, an immoral news media, the costly military industrial complex, an unelected Federal Reserve, and a rigged financial system which are rapidly taking away precious freedoms, destroying lives in countless ways, and making ordinary citizens poorer by the day through gross mismanagement and highly destructive policies.

The American citizens need to abandon the two political parties which benefit from dividing Americans, and band together as a unified group to take back this country from their oppressors in the tyrannical ruling class. It is time for an American political revolution.

The fundamental problem with the attack on the United States Capital on January 6, 2021, remains that this was a partisan event, and was easily characterized as such by the ruling class in Washington.[119]

If this was a nonpartisan and unified rejection of our corrupt

---

[119] The event is often characterized as a demonstration or attack on the Capital depending upon political affiliation, particular agenda, and overall motivation.

and incompetent government policies and thoroughly broken political system, then it becomes a legitimate revolution by the American people and stands as a patriotic freedom movement.[120]

All Americans should be united more than ever before, reject the temptation of partisan politics, as everyone in this country is losing individual freedoms at an alarming rate, and if partisan censorship prevails, in the end, it can be applied to whichever group isn't in political power. Hence, all political censorship is bad for America.

There has been a tremendous whittling away of individual thought and free speech in America that started with the slippery slope of political correctness, enthusiastically leading to language and word shaming, which invariably brought in the imperial thought police, ushered in the unenlightened era of cancel culture, and ultimately, we ended up with massive censorship and losing freedom of speech as treasured ideals and once sacred ground in our forlornly fading democracy.

Let the free marketplace reward good ideas and punish bad ideas in our society, we don't need government or large technology companies dictating the marketplace of ideas. Having freedom of thought and speech, even if it offends people, is essential in a true democracy.

Once America ventured down the limitless rabbit hole of hate speech and hate crimes this really opened up a perniciously stifling Pandora's box in trying to control people's minds and thoughts via the authoritarian state and an ever more intrusively domineering government. *You must conform to every aspect of our*

---

[120] https://en.wikipedia.org/wiki/2021_United_States_Capitol_attack; https://www.history.com/this-day-in-history/january-6-capitol-riot

*political ideology!*

In principle, there is no such thing as hate crimes in the external world, apart from political beliefs, and you end up devaluing a material nature of the crime itself, by trying to politicize it.[121] Ironically, this only leads to more hate crimes in society.

As a practical matter, we cannot legislate hate, hate is a rather complicated emotional state of the brain, it is not the role of government to try and control/regulate complex emotions produced by the brain.

In a free world, people are allowed to have a range of natural human emotions such as hate. This is a particularly futile game played by the ruling class. Next, our authoritarian government will be controlling, regulating, and taxing the notion of love.

Indeed, the government lunacy here is palpable, have there ever been any love crimes? *"Oh, I loved her to death officer!"* The act of crime is bad enough, and stands on its own merits, it doesn't require anything else being added to the equation, such as psychological motivation or interpretation of brain states.

Fundamentally, this is politicizing crime, speech and thought. Once the government starts dictating and legislating what its citizens think, you are well on your way to losing all individual freedoms, it is just a matter of time.

We are witnessing an increasingly intrusive and tyrannical government with each passing year, and it is vitally important

---

[121] I understand that there are state and federal hate crime laws, this philosophical discussion merely points out the slippery slope of unintended consequences which inevitably plays out when big government starts politicizing important objective and theoretically nonpartisan areas of society such as our legal and judicial systems. We are also experiencing this similar slippery slope vis-à-vis the persistent promotion of various political ideologies within our failing education system right now.

for Americans to identify the real enemies, wake up from their partisan slumber, and stop behaving like moronic multitudes of mindless sheep.

It is time for the American people to wake up and start fighting for their freedoms once again. This ideological and philosophical fight must be undertaken with great ferocity before it is entirely too late, as we need to stop this steep decline in the once cherished and traditional American values representative of true liberty, freedom of speech and thought, and inherent individual rights which are absolutely necessary in any legitimate representative democracy.

The American people should demand a strict adherence, an unequivocal respect, and an undying preservation of these core founding values from their tax supported government leaders and institutions, as a basic nonnegotiable starting point for the Democracy.

It is quite apparent that as government has gotten bigger and more intrusive in dominating our lives, we have lost more freedoms as individuals along the way. This relationship will continue so long as the citizenry agrees to this political subjugation by big government.

In actuality, the biggest threat to our democracy is not Russia, or even China for that matter, and it sure isn't the bogeyman of domestic terrorism that is a popular refrain these days, the biggest threat to the United States of America is our corrupt and incompetent government which has been actively destroying this great nation for the last 70 years.

Our rotten government has done far more damage than any foreign competitors or nations. In truth, the ruling class in America has been destroying the country from within through terribly corrupt and inept government policies. Consequently, our biggest threat isn't domestic terrorism, it is domestic government.

In other words, our failing republic is experiencing a significantly steep decline on the global stage because foreign nations have been managed and run far better than America over the last 70 years. In point of fact, our sheer incompetence and poor management will bring down this struggling and severely weakened representative democracy far sooner than China could ever hope to accomplish from a strategic standpoint.

Instead of putting a literal fence around the Capital to protect lawmakers from the citizenry, we need to build a philosophical ethics and sound judgement wall around the Capital to protect everyday Americans from our corrupt and incompetent politicians and their grievously destructive government policies.

In all honesty, we would be better served by locking up and imprisoning the career politicians and corrupt bureaucrats in Washington versus letting these political grifters continue to irrevocably destroy this country. These card-carrying criminals are the real threats standing in the way of America having a legitimate representative democracy.

It is obvious that we don't live in a legitimate Democracy right now, the government's main objectives are the following: continuing to get bigger, gaining additional powers, controlling more aspects of its citizens lives, taxing everything that moves, and systematically destroying personal freedoms at an increasingly alarming rate with little regard for the consequences.

Fundamentally, we have an illegitimate, nonrepresentative tyrannical government masquerading as a true democracy.

Just look up the definitions for freedom and democracy and ask yourself if this is the America that our Founding Fathers envisioned when they escaped the government tyranny of Great Britain.[122]

Candidly, America isn't even the same country that I grew up in as a child, I can only imagine what the Founding Fathers would think of our professed representative democracy today.

America really has lost its way in many areas at this critical juncture in history, such as preserving our inherent rights towards freedom of speech and protecting our important individual liberties and freedoms from despotic government overreach.

Just as a reminder of our foundational past I include the following from the Declaration of Independence:

> When in the Course of human events, it becomes necessary for one people to dissolve the political bands which have connected them with another, and to assume among the powers of the earth, the separate and equal station to which the Laws of Nature and of Nature's God entitle them, a decent respect to the opinions of mankind requires that they should declare the causes which impel them to the separation. We hold these truths to be self-evident, that all men are created equal, that they are endowed by their Creator with certain unalienable Rights, that among these are Life, Liberty and the pursuit of Happiness. That to secure these rights,

---

[122] https://www.britannica.com/topic/Founding-Fathers; https://en.wikipedia.org/wiki/Founding_Fathers_of_the_United_States; https://www.history.com/topics/american-revolution/founding-fathers-united-states

Governments are instituted among Men, deriving their just powers from the consent of the governed, that whenever any Form of Government becomes destructive of these ends, it is the Right of the People to alter or to abolish it, and to institute new Government, laying its foundation on such principles and organizing its powers in such form, as to them shall seem most likely to effect their Safety and Happiness. Prudence, indeed, will dictate that Governments long established should not be changed for light and transient causes; and accordingly all experience hath shewn, that mankind are more disposed to suffer, while evils are sufferable, than to right themselves by abolishing the forms to which they are accustomed. But when a long train of abuses and usurpations, pursuing invariably the same Object evinces a design to reduce them under absolute Despotism, it is their right, it is their duty, to throw off such Government, and to provide new Guards for their future security. Such has been the patient sufferance of these Colonies; and such is now the necessity which constrains them to alter their former Systems of Government. The history of the present King of Great Britain is a history of repeated injuries and usurpations, all having in direct object the establishment of an absolute Tyranny over these States. To prove this, let Facts be submitted to a candid world.[123]

---

[123] Excerpt taken from The Declaration of Independence, Action of Second Continental Congress, July 4, 1776, The Unanimous Declaration of the thirteen united States of America.
https://www.archives.gov/founding-docs/declaration-transcript;
https://www.uscis.gov/sites/default/files/document/guides/M-654.pdf

When a government starts taking away basic freedoms from its citizens, especially freedoms which are necessary for any legitimate democracy, then it is time for an American Political Revolution.

John Mark Gray

# ABOUT THE AUTHOR

John Mark Gray has a MA in Philosophy and an MBA in Business. He has worked in academia, Fortune 500 companies, consulting, and financial markets. He has written many articles and white papers on financial markets and economics. He has a background in Logic & Game Theory and enjoys playing Chess and Poker in his spare time.

www.ingramcontent.com/pod-product-compliance
Lightning Source LLC
Chambersburg PA
CBHW031116250726
48655CB00004B/1739